ARCHITECTURAL
GUIDES FOR TRAVELERS
·
MEDIEVAL
TUSCANY
AND UMBRIA

To Laura

ARCHITECTURAL
GUIDES FOR TRAVELERS

•

MEDIEVAL TUSCANY AND UMBRIA

ANTHONY OSLER McINTYRE

CHRONICLE BOOKS • SAN FRANCISCO

First published in the United States in 1992 by Chronicle Books

Copyright 1992 by Garden House Editions Ltd., London.
Text copyright: Anthony Osler McIntyre hereby asserts and gives notice of his right under section 77 of the Copyright, Designs and Patents Act 1988 to be identified as author of the text of this book. © Anthony Osler McIntyre 1992.

Series conceived by Georgina Harding
Editor: Elisabeth Ingles
Managing editor: Louisa McDonnell
Series design: Clare Finlaison
Design: Wendy Bann
Maps and plans: David Woodroffe
Picture research: Nicholas Shaddick
Index: Hilary Bird

Printed in England by Jolly & Barber Ltd., Rugby, Warks

Library of Congress Cataloging-in-Publication Data
McIntyre, Anthony
  Medieval Tuscany and Umbria/by Anthony Osler McIntyre.
  p. cm.—(Architectural guides for travelers)
  Includes bibliographical references and index.
  ISBN 0–87701–846–4
  1. Architecture, Medieval—Italy—Tuscany. 2. Architecture—Italy—Tuscany.
  3. Architecture, Medieval—Italy—Umbria. 4. Architecture—Italy—Umbria.
  I. Title. II. Series.
NA1119.T8M37 1992
720'945'50902—dc20   91——32843
                                                              CIP

10 9 8 7 6 5 4 3 2 1

Chronicle Books
275 Fifth Street
San Francisco, California 94103

CONTENTS

PREFACE

The ideal guide book for travellers has somehow to provide for the differing sequences of history and geography. This guide deals with the historical sequence by starting with an essay that outlines the main political and social events of medieval times, events that might be said to make up an 'invisible context' of architecture. Following that is a series of eight chapters, starting with the towns and cities of north-west Tuscany and ending with those of Umbria to the east; each forms a small architectural itinerary. Buildings have been arranged so that their appearance in the text corresponds as far as possible to convenient road routes. The regional maps at the head of each section should make this clear. Although it seems somewhat arbitrary to give 'touring days required' for these itineraries, three or four days should be enough to get round the buildings described in each of the eight areas.

This guide is of course selective. Every century has left us works of high quality, from the pre-Roman Etruscans to the Renaissance and right into our own century. It would take a determined individual to walk the streets of Florence and see only medieval buildings, or to drive through Umbria and not be deeply impressed by the landscape. My hope is that people will use this guide as a magnifying glass – however weak a one it may be – to study particular details of a beautiful country and a great civilization.

(*Opposite*) The Palazzo Pubblico and the Torre del Mangia in the Campo of Siena.

INTRODUCTION

Any traveller interested in medieval architecture could scarcely imagine a paradise richer than Tuscany and Umbria, whose cities, towns and villages are redolent of their glory days in the late Middle Ages. The sheer abundance of these sites, some grand and famous but many of them quite small, means that a wealth of fine towns and monuments can be found well away from the beaten track: ideal places for a relaxed day's outing.

The greater proportion of medieval construction has of course vanished: walls, narrow streets, the tower houses that proliferated not only in San Gimignano but in Florence, Pisa and Siena. Few places have more than fragmentary remains of these essential features of the medieval city. Not surprisingly the larger and more active cities have suffered most: Florence, beautiful as it may be, was largely rebuilt in the 19th century. This was partly done for the sake of 'modernization', but partly too in order to exaggerate the importance of its Renaissance monuments. Consequently Florence, while it has many fine medieval buildings, has little of the medieval atmosphere to be found in some of the smaller cities like Gubbio, Assisi and Orvieto, that maintain almost intact the character given to them by their builders of the late Middle Ages.

Like most names coined to label historic periods, the term *medieval* was meant as a snipe at the past. To people of the Renaissance, the period between the end of the Roman Empire in the fifth century and the humanism of the 15th century was one of ignorance, darkness and confusion, when the standards of arts, politics and intellectual life fell far below those of classical times. Historians generally use 'Middle Ages' to refer to that period between the abdication of the last Roman Emperor in the West, Romulus Augustulus, in 476, and the fall of Constantinople in 1453. However the term *medieval* was

(Opposite) St Francis casts out the Demons from Arezzo. Fresco by Giotto in San Francesco, Assisi.

1

invented in the 16th century to describe what was then regarded as a hiatus between the classical traditions of ancient and Renaissance times: a millennium of decadence and decay. This was a very convenient philosophy for an age that saw itself as linked to the classical past. By inventing a 'middle ages', Renaissance man had invented a past he could reject with a clear conscience.

Yet if the men of the 15th century were clear about what they meant by the Middle Ages, today we are less so. A thousand years of history is a long time. The unified character of the period, if ever obvious to the Renaissance, is not at all clear to us. An age that encompasses the rise and fall of feudalism; the Carolingian, Papal and Holy Roman Empires; the growth of nation-states in England and France; the creation of Romanesque and Gothic architectures; the Crusades — it is hard to see where all these phenomena overlap to become 'medieval'.

Modern historians have been tracing the roots of the Renaissance farther and farther back, into the 13th century, into the 12th and 11th. But what roots are these? They are in fact an integral part of the Renaissance itself, and in a much broader sense than art-history would suggest. The West's invasion of the Near East during the Crusades was very much the same thing as the earlier Hellenic and Roman pillaging of more skilled, highly cultured and ancient civilizations. We may not care to recognize the work of destruction that preceded the achievements of the *quattrocento*, but it was considerable and extensive. That it happened outside Europe makes it easier to ignore. Yet the organized violence between Italian states was brutal enough, and if the aesthetic of many of the public buildings was stark and harsh, it is because these were rough times: it cannot be an exaggeration to say that for every building the Florentines put up they knocked down three. This was not just to clear the site for prettier things. It was their policy to destroy the castles and towns of their enemies — in fact competitors in trade and agricultural wealth. In 1125 Florence began a century of violent destruction with the complete eradication of all civic buildings in the neighbouring city of Fiesole. Their opponents were trying to do the same to them; the destructive tendency was part of the age.

Since we are here concerned with describing architecture that can still be seen, the dilemma as to what is medieval becomes less relevant. We have only three architectural styles to deal with: Byzantine, Romanesque and Gothic. The first is marginal to Tusco-Umbrian architectural history. Instead of a thousand years of building, we see less than half of that, a period of production that starts in the 11th century and ends, it may be said, in the first decades of the 15th, when the Gothic body of the Duomo in Florence is hatted with Brunelleschi's classicizing dome.

What we find, in fact, is another renaissance, taking place well in advance of the classical one. We find a social rebirth, a growth of cities after their gradual depopulation from the fifth to the tenth centuries, and a parallel growth in the institutions and mechanisms that necessarily accompany urban life. What we now consider the classical Renaissance flowered on much older stock.

The historical and artistic background

If the city was once again found to be a useful social and economic proposition in late medieval times, nowhere was its development more thorough and of such artistic importance as in the central Italian regions of Tuscany and Umbria. It was here that independent city-states flowered once more, as they had done in Etruscan times. (Legend relates the story of Romulus calling on the Etruscans, the experts in these affairs, to organize the foundation rites for the city of Rome itself.) Trade routes opened up by the first Crusades in the late 11th century were rapidly exploited by towns such as Pisa, which established trading colonies in the Levant, and by Siena and Florence, which were soon to become the world's first banking cities. Intense competition between trading towns meant that defensive walls had to be built. These reinforced the urban idea and gave its boundaries precise definition, but also confined the space available on the ground for development. Judicious use had to be made of the enclosed space: the art of city planning developed.

The Adoration of the Magi by Bartolo di Fredi: detail of the town of Siena (Pinacoteca, Siena).

This last point may seem unexpected, even doubtful. The high romance of towns such as Siena, Gubbio, Orvieto, we imagine to be the result of happy accident, the rambling workings of the medieval mind. But no: throughout the period under discussion, men became increasingly adept at combining the natural advantages of the land with the ever more complex requirements of city architecture. Without arriving at later notions of ideal city planning, where the whole was conceived at one time, the medieval architects learned how to incorporate the valuable existing fabric of their cities into new projects. Rules and regulations were developed, not as absolutes, but as fitting particular circumstances. For this was a time of transition, when the artisan was developing into the artist and asserting intellectual as well as manual ambitions. Architects like Arnolfo di Cambio, Angelo da Orvieto and Matteo Gattapone emerged as great and unique artists, sought out and given commissions throughout central Italy.

Medieval Italian history was formed along two axes. In the fifth century, ties between Byzantium and Rome were still strong, and the East-West axis was the line along which political as well as ecclesiastical power moved. Over the next thousand years, through religious disputes and local warfare, that axis was to be broken. In its place, a new political bond was tied between the Italian states and the north of Europe. Yet it was only after the political link with Byzantium had been weakened beyond repair, and largely as a result of its weakness, that significant trade routes could be established between East and West. After the 11th century Italian merchants, backed by a strong

Donkeys leaving the gates of Colle Val d'Elsa with bags full of grain towards Pisa, empty towards Florence. Miniature from the Biadajolo (Biblioteca Laurenziana, Florence).

papacy and with powerful fleets of their own, could challenge Byzantium's trade monopoly.

This trade was both commercial and technical, and the two were intimately connected. There is little doubt that the Crusades had as great an effect on European technology as they did on commercial trading. From the introduction of Arabic numerals (really Indian, by way of Arabia) by the Pisan mathematician Fibonacci in 1201, to the more humble wheelbarrow, a Chinese invention first found on European building sites in the 13th century, the technical traffic was all one way, and had a most profound influence on the course of western civilization.

The city

The real achievement of late medieval architecture in Tuscany and Umbria was the development of the city as a functional element of civilization. Partly this means the city's development as a mechanism for trading: warehouse, market, meeting place, all secure behind heavy walls. But in Italy it was always more than that, and the strong traditions of city life in Roman times and earlier never entirely died out. Landowners as well as merchants were the residents of medieval cities. What they lacked until the 13th century was any political or administrative role, because these functions had been removed away from the cities, into castles and foreign capitals.

The medieval city is a thing so different from what we today call cities that a word or two of explanation is necessary. Our cities are full of tall office blocks and are gate-less, wall-less entities: the drive-in city. Eight and nine hundred years ago a city was like a well-fortified house, with strong doors and thick walls, and it was locked up at night.

Walls and fortifications

First and foremost a medieval city had walls. Many of those discussed in this book were originally Etruscan and Roman cities – Florence, Lucca, Arezzo – whose populations had diminished during the Dark Ages. And although they became devoid of the functions of government, they were still liked as places to live in by people of all classes; so that, when the population of Europe began to increase from the tenth century, urban centres naturally grew with a revival of trade, manufacture and agriculture. They almost always started with a physical inheritance of walls and plans – the gates, streets and open places – from Roman times.

Fortification played an important part in the development of medieval cities. After the middle of the 11th century attacks on towns became more sophisticated than the simple looting raids of earlier times. Neighbouring cities were now out to raze competing towns and take over their territory. This was the moment of renaissance for the classical siege, when armies would sit down before the walls and use their patience and cunning, as well as their strength, to winkle out the citizens. Good defences became vitally important.

Foreign invasions of Italy meant foreign feudal lords, just as in England feudal lords were Normans among a Saxon population. They were not especially welcome, and the houses they built for themselves were fortified as castles, always outside a city's walls. In Tuscany the issue is clouded somewhat by the fact that a fortified village is often called *castello*. *Rocca* on the whole refers to a citadel, not, in other words, a house, but rather a defended garrison post, generally high up on a hill or promontory, a place hard of access. Most medieval castles and citadels were destroyed before the 14th century by warring cities. The Rocce that exist in so many cities today were mostly built in the 15th and 16th centuries to enforce loyalty to pope or Tuscan duke.

Walls could keep enemies at bay but they served another purpose as well. No goods could enter or leave without passing through a gate, so the walls were a means of regulating supply and raising duties. But as towns prospered, merchants, traders and goods would congregate around the gates, taking the risk of staying outside the walls, creating markets where there was space and where the cost of trading was less. In France these clusters of dwellings outside the town walls were called *faubourgs*,

The medieval walls of
Florence.
- – – – Roman walls
- . . . . Walls of the
  Byzantine
  city
- – · – · – Expansion of
  the 8th–9th
  centuries
- ——— Walls at the
  end of the
  12th century

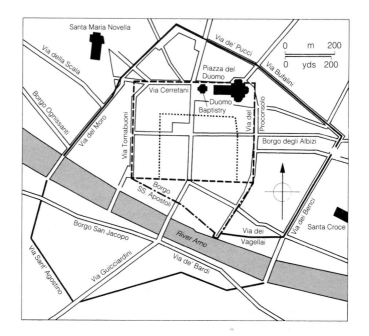

the town itself being the *bourg*. But in Italy the city was, in Roman tradition, called *civitas*, and *borgo*, or *sobborgo*, always referred to these new developments outside the walls. In time, the *borghi* had enough power and importance to claim the city's rights and protection, and new circles of walls were built to include them.

What **Florence** lacks in medieval atmosphere it makes up for in the clarity of its historical development: in no other city in central Italy is the development of the plan so well documented or so instructive. The plan above shows the original Roman walls, and the smaller Byzantine enclosure within them. Between the eighth and ninth centuries an extension was made on the southern side to include a gate on the Arno. Each quarter of the city had its own administrative identity, and each was named after one of the four gates. But at the end of the 12th century the *borghi* on all four sides had grown, and were enclosed by a new wall. And look how it is built, not parallel to the old walls, but rotated through 45°: the new town had clearly developed round the gates. Bigger walls, more

8

gates: the city was becoming richer and more diverse. The four *quartieri* were replaced by six *sestieri*. Soon these new walls proved too tight a fit, and the final enclosure was built much farther out, returning the orientation more or less to that of the Roman city. These successive wallings can still be traced out in the modern streets, and are set out in the pages on Florence that follow.

The piazza

If the walls of a city were its first requirement, its public spaces were no less important. For the city was established as the place of exchange, and the desire to exchange and acquire ideas as well as objects that brings the city into being. The central Italian town typically has three important piazzas: religious, political and trading. Sometimes the three are interconnected, as at San Gimignano and Pistoia, to form a sequence of city spaces. More commonly, as at Orvieto and Lucca, they were located in different parts of the city.

The *piazza del Duomo* was used for church festivals and ceremonies. It has a particular character, often isolated behind the main thoroughfares where the civic piazzas thrived. The main churches did not normally require a large forecourt, for the space within these buildings was, even as late as the 18th century, often as large as a piazza. People gathered within the building to hear and see religious events, while the piazza was used for the beginning and end of open-air processions. Another factor here was space. The Duomo, usually the oldest church in a city, would stand within the oldest walls, where space was at a premium. The late mendicant churches were built outside those old walls, and follow different rules.

The *piazza del comune* (known by various names, such as the Piazza della Signoria, Piazza del Podestà, Piazza del Comune, Piazza del Popolo, and so on, according to the name of the civic building fronting it) was a place organized specifically around the government of city life. Here civic processions would begin, here the *carroccio* would be brought, the great military cart with its bell and flags, rallying point for a city's army in battle. Siena's famous Palio takes place in its Piazza del Campo: that miraculous space, 'the definitive image of what the modern city has slowly lost', as Enrico Guidoni wrote, 'the central space dedicated to public processions and events, and to the development of a direct dialogue between the organs of government and the totality of the population.' Once each city had many such events as the Palio, games organized within the city in which the different *contrade*, or districts, competed.

The Campo at Siena lay outside the walls until the 12th century. Originally the Campo dei Fiori, it served as a market-place until late medieval times. This fact shows the way that markets developed, starting within the old walls, as the Mercato Vecchio in Florence, gradually being supplanted by the newer markets growing up outside the gates. Most of these market squares are known by the names of the mendicant churches that were built beside them. Locate a Piazza Sant' Agostino, or San Domenico, or San Francesco, and you have almost certainly found an old market-place.

The growing importance of the *piazza del comune* – and there were two in many cities – from the 12th century, and its culmination in the 13th and 14th centuries with the spectacular examples of Siena and Gubbio, is an indication of the rapid development and refinement of civic government and the artistic sophistication it both promoted and harnessed.

Public and religious institutions and buildings

The walls of the city tended to follow the Roman originals and the same is true of its plan. The Mercato Vecchio in Florence, now the Piazza della Repubblica, occupied the site of the Roman forum (though the medieval buildings were mostly destroyed in the 19th century), and the same is true at Orvieto. The typical cross streets of the Roman plan remain in Florence, *cardo* and *decumanus*. Houses were rebuilt on old street patterns, while new developments, particularly the large monasteries and churches, were built on virgin sites outside the walls. Major

buildings within the old walls tended to occupy the same sites even when one culture replaced another, such as the Baptistry at Florence, standing on the site – indeed on the very foundations – of a classical structure. Not only did the ancient public buildings provide large sites at a time when the means of legal expropriation were almost non-existent, they also provided quarries of building material. Significantly, a Florentine enterprise like the building of the Palazzo della Signoria (Palazzo Vecchio) in 1299, which involved the demolition of many buildings, was made possible because the Uberti family who owned the land had been exiled from the city and their houses stood empty.

The 'Catena' view of Florence, about 1490. Woodcut.

And here is another important factor in medieval urban development. Families tended to build up a number of houses in a quarter of the town, so that family enclaves were formed. In these times of civil wars and feuding, there were defensive advantages to these groupings. The Case dei Guinigi in Lucca are the remains of such a development. It was precisely this close packing of family property that made possible the redevelopment of large areas in Renaissance times, when the many small houses in one family's ownership could be demolished and a single massive palazzo built to take their place.

In every city we find buildings called the Palazzo Comune, Palazzo della Signoria, or Palazzo Pubblico;

Podestà, Bargello, or Palazzo del Capitano, prominent and splendid structures. Today they often house civic art galleries and museums, but what were they built for, what institutions did they house eight hundred years ago?

The cities of Tuscany were unique in European history. In the endless war between the papacy and the Holy Roman Empire that followed the death of Charlemagne in the ninth century, northern Italy became a battlefield, and the loyalty of its cities was demanded by both sides. **Guelph** and **Ghibelline** factions formed, supporting pope and emperor, their names being Italianized versions of German tags. (The easiest way of remembering which is which is that 'Guelph' and 'pope' are the short words, 'Ghibelline' and 'empire' the long.) During the 11th century, when the **Countess Matilda** ruled Tuscany, she was assisted by a group of feudal nobles, lawyers and judges, who were known as *sapientes*, or *boni homines*. Matilda's frequent absences from her cities gave these assistants virtual rulership, and prepared the way for the government of the communes, or city councils, which developed rapidly when it became clear that neither pope nor empire was in full control.

Matilda, who herself had been given a good education and encouraged literature and the arts in her own court, was a fervent Guelph supporter, and this was hardly surprising since the Emperor Henry IV had caused the murder of her father. Before her death she gave her extensive lands – most of Tuscany – to the pope. Naturally her assistants, her *boni homines*, themselves tended to favour the pope's cause. Upon Matilda's death in 1115 these groups continued to rule, but now they did so in the name of the people.

There is a tendency to romanticize the **communes** as early forms of democratic government, but the truth is somewhat different. They were city councils formed in a variety of circumstances, but essentially as expedient political and administrative organizations, taking the initiative at a time when the administrative structure of the empire was too weak to resist. Neither was the commune the victory of bourgeoisie over aristocratic landowner. The city housed both these groups, and both vied for power. Sometimes they divided these powers and at other times they fought each other for them. It was indeed the nobility who became known as the *torri*, or the people with the towers, from the tall defensive structures they built within the city walls in almost all central Italian cities. San Gimignano is the sparse surviving representative of these forest-like cities. Opposing the torri were the *arti*, members of trade and merchant guilds. Again, these were not the petty artisans, but the wealthy manufacturers and bankers. In principle government was open to all, in practice it was soon enough concentrated in the hands of a few families. Yet one should not be overly cynical about these events, for the principle of democratic government had been established.

In the 13th century most communes developed into a legislature that was elected annually, with no member being allowed re-election. This was meant to make it difficult for any single political or social group to gain control, although over the centuries there was a tendency to extend tenure and undermine the democratic nature of the commune, until its final reduction in the 15th century to a passive body, as tyrannical regimes took over.

City against city may have been a matter of domination of trade routes and markets, but within each city-state, battles for power were no less seriously fought. The merchant and artisan class, whose efforts were enriching the cities, tended to side with the pope. In a politically fragmented and volatile Europe, the Church was the only unifying element, and provided the merchants with a useful 'foreign embassy' abroad. Indeed, on the one occasion that the pope withdrew his support for the Sienese bankers – by excommunicating the whole population – the results were disastrous: debtors claimed they had no obligation to pay those whom the pope had condemned.

On the other hand trade routes needed defending, the *contado* needed enlarging and enemies needed crushing. All these needs could only be satisfied with military force, and leadership in this was the role of the nobility. They quite naturally sided with their feudal lord, the emperor. Such were the intrigues and arguments between these factions within communes that the office of *podestà* was introduced, filled at first by a member of the nobility but later always by a *forestiero*, a stranger whose detachment from the city's interests was meant to ensure impartiality. It was the *podestà*'s job, as head of the commune, to ensure justice in disputes and maintain the peace between disputing factions. His instrument of 'public security' was an officer called the *bargello*, often used by the *podestà* to settle personal political scores: an unloved figure.

The citizens themselves had military duties, both defensive and offensive, under the *capitano del popolo*. They were foot soldiers, armed with long pikes, who could take on the cavalry of an imperial force or the *condottieri*. After the mid-13th century the military was led by a number of *gonfalonieri*, or standard-bearers (twelve in the case of Florence: three for each quarter, or 'gate'). Together with the *Priori delle Arti* these men formed the organ of central government, the *Signoria*.

Architecture and Sculpture. Bas-reliefs by Andrea Pisano on the Campanile of the Duomo, Florence, 1337–43.

But the radically new components of medieval city government were the *arti*, the craft, trade and merchant guilds. Now a source of wealth that rivalled that of agriculture, the *arti* gained political power. If a modern equivalent had to be found it would probably be the Institute of Directors rather than the trade unions. They included artisans as well as merchants, but 'artisan' might mean someone who owned silk-weaving factories. The power of the *arti* was opposed to that of the nobility, militarily weaker but their economic resources more potent and more mobile. They could, after all, hire mercenaries if need be to fight for their interests. It was the high level of organization within these *arti* that kept the cities, and most particularly Florence, running as commercial enterprises throughout periods of enormous political and social upheaval – cities that occasionally had no government at all.

The *arti* did not, on the whole, build great palaces for their own use. Instead they sponsored public buildings, and so in Florence the *Arte della Lana*, the wool-merchants' guild, was responsible for the cathedral, while Ghiberti's baptistry doors were provided by the *Arte dei Mercanti*.

The definitions given above must be allowed some elasticity, as in both time and place their meanings are liable to change. At one moment the *comune* would be led by the *podestà*, while the *capitano* would control the *popolo*, as happened in Florence in the mid-13th century. At another the *podestà* would be the emperor's tool, with *gonfalonieri* running the popular movement. But these terms should provide at least some grasp of the main functioning elements of late medieval politics in the Tuscan and Umbrian cities.

Monasteries

Other medieval institutions are more familiar. Monasticism, an Egyptian and Syrian religious notion, was developed in sixth-century western Europe by **St Benedict**, who submitted Eastern spiritual ideas to the discipline of Roman organization. In the following centuries the Benedictine rule spread from Montecassino throughout western Christendom, carrying with it, in the early Middle Ages when secular government was at its lowest ebb, the ideal and practice of community government. The movement received a substantial boost when some 50,000 Syrian monks left the Near East in the eighth century because of religious disputes, and settled in Italy.

Medieval monasteries were as large as most towns, with the difference that they had governments and administrative organizations at a time when towns had none. The monastic settlements maintained libraries, taught, cared for the sick and the needy, blending ideals of civic and spiritual responsibility, the classical and Christian worlds. When someone like Pugin in the 19th century looked longingly back to medieval institutions and promoted their revival, the organizations he was admiring, if not their principles, were largely classical.

The Benedictines increasingly devoted themselves to prayer. Over the years they extended their services and multiplied their offices of prayer, and yet still their communities prospered. Two developments accounted for this. One was the increased use of lay-brothers to work the land, men who did not participate in the elaborate spiritual exercises. (As a side-benefit this undoubtedly increased the monks' administrative talents.) Another was the increased use of mechanization, such as the efficient harnessing of water power. It would be many years before medieval secular civilization caught up with the technical and administrative capabilities of the Benedictine houses, although the monasteries did act as universities, taking in the sons of the richer merchants and nobility, and passing on their skills.

Some of the Benedictines also increasingly devoted themselves to the worldly life, the life of the wealthy landlord. Theirs was virtually the only monastic rule in existence until in the 11th century some monks, dissatisfied with the low level of spirituality among their Benedictine brothers, broke away to set up their own community at Cîteaux. **St Bernard** in the next century turned this into the first monastic order – a parent institution to many others, all under exactly the same rules. Reactionary or revolutionary, the Cistercians returned to a literal observation of St Benedict's rule, with particular emphasis on working the land. Their dedication in farming virgin land led to a significant increase in the agricultural capacity of medieval society, itself a concomitant of urban growth. It also led, with bequests and tithes, to their monasteries becoming richer and more powerful than those of the Benedictines.

But these orders were soon joined by others with very different principles. While the Benedictines and the Cistercians were usually to be found in the country, their survival being based on economic autonomy, the new orders were by necessity in or adjacent to towns and cities. These were the mendicant or begging orders, and the first of them was the Franciscan order, sanctioned in 1209 by Innocent III. The principles of **St Francis** demonstrate more clearly than any other phenomenon the radical difference between the classical and the Christian worlds. Nothing, in classical times, could be worse than poverty. It may have been a mark of refinement to give alms, but it was plain bad luck to be poor. Yet the Franciscans embraced poverty and preached it as a virtue: and they were immensely successful.

Because of their early start, the Benedictines often have churches within the oldest walls of the medieval cities, but the mendicant orders – Franciscans, Augustinians, Dominicans, Carmelites and Servites – were not founded until the 13th century, and had therefore to take their places outside the old walls, in the *borghi*. And this is where they were needed, among the new city population of the artisans excluded from the traditional order of things, where the mendicants could best represent the positive values of religious discipline and humanism. We tend to think of the mendicants as literally 'begging orders', which is indeed the meaning of the word. St Francis's idea was simply thatt his friars should live by their own effortts, and have no possessions, living always with no thought for the future. In this way they differed little fromm the artisans among whom they lived. Their buildings, with large churches for preaching to the population, were frequently sited beside the *borgo* market squares, which remain to this day. Examples are the piazzas of Santa Croce and del Carmine in Florence, and San Domenico in Perugia.

St Francis renounces his Possessions. Detail of fresco by Giotto in San Francesco, Assisi.

A detail might be mentioned here in order to convey to a sceptical age something of the religious and social feeling of medieval society. It was not infrequent for medieval businesses, normally an association of capital investors, to include God himself as a partner in an investment enterprise and to credit Him with a capital sum. Though He had of course not actually invested anything, when profits were being divided He was entitled to His share, which went to charity.

Medieval architecture in Tuscany and Umbria

By far the greater part of what was built in medieval times has disappeared, and most of what does remain dates from the 13th and 14th centuries. Earlier work was usually built in wood, and when of stone was eventually demolished to make way for newer buildings in a more refined style of architecture. It is mostly these monumental buildings that are left to us, built in one of two great architectural manners, the Romanesque and the Gothic, and sometimes in a combination of the two.

The name **Romanesque** indicates the style's debt to classical architecture. As a living architecture it was partly an inheritance from the Lombards, who had ruled in Central Italy until the eighth century, and to some extent from the Carolingian architects who had followed them. Yet the medieval artist grew up surrounded by real classical buildings, as were so many of the structures he demolished to build the new civic palaces or churches.

In its French manifestation, the Romanesque is an immensely weighty, solid and solemn architecture. In Tuscany things were different, and if architectural styles were to be identified not by formal criteria – the shape of the arches, the vaulting, the plan types – but by their abstract qualities, then it would be hard to put this Italian Romanesque in the same category as its French, English, Spanish and German counterparts. For this, at least in its marble-covered guise, is an architecture not so much of weight and solidity as of volume and surface.

A look at the Badia at Fiesole gives something of the idea. Here, a small and delicate marble façade, built around 1025, sits at the foot of a much larger wall of bare brickwork, in which scaffolding pockets are still visible. It does not matter that the brick wall was built later than the marble one: the idea is there, the manner of construction is plain, the sense that *the brick is heavy* and *the marble is surface decoration*. The Tuscan works are all built like this. The preferred material early on was brick: cheap, easy to handle and quick. Unlike the Po Valley, however, Tuscany and Umbria are well provided with good building stone, which was increasingly employed in the 12th and 13th centuries.

Having said that, it must be made clear that the Romanesque was a style based on 'wearing grandfather's clothes'. The past was a rich scrap-heap: arch form, vaulting and mass walling were all re-used, but more strikingly. Many pieces of ancient buildings were also incorporated directly, in particular columns and capitals, the former of which were beyond the means of medieval masons. Pisa's cathedral has two splendid rows, and the basilica of San Salvatore at Spoleto is almost wholly made of antique fragments. These were the building blocks with

Florence: the Badia Fiesolana – the old façade set into the new.

which medieval architecture played in its infancy.

The Romanesque is first seen at the Baptistry of San Giovanni in Florence (consecrated 1059), where each of its eight walls is given a high round-headed arch – the Roman arch – like 'a Roman stone aqueduct bent around eight angles', in Kenneth Conant's description. However it lacks the secondary and tertiary arcading of the classical aqueduct, which was in fact characteristic of much Romanesque work. But the proportioning and detailing are pretty thoroughly classical, and it has been pointed out that since the baptistry has at one time or another been ascribed to every century from the fourth to the 12th, it can certainly be said to carry the spirit of classicism. Its external decoration is a veneer of strongly contrasting dark-green and white marbles over solid structural masonry. The zebra-work on its eight corners, however, so typical of later Gothic work, was done in the 13th century under the influence of the characteristic Pisan architecture.

The cathedral complex at **Pisa** is one of the most magnificent of all Romanesque compositions. In the 11th century the Pisans had formed an alliance with the Normans to drive the Saracens from Sicily. The Normans dropping out at the last minute, the Pisan navy went on alone, conquering the opposing fleet, and the proceeds from part of the booty were devoted to the building of their newly begun cathedral. This, together with the baptistry (1153), campanile (1174) and Campo Santo or cemetery (1278), forms one of the great Romanesque monumental groupings, which, moreover, shows us all the elements of Roman architecture that the Romanesque adopted. The cathedral plan is in a sense the standard nave-and-transepts arrangement. Closer study, and a look at the elevations, shows something much more like three basilicas surrounding the central crossing. The building also illustrates, with its marble decoration, the Tuscans' desire to make their massive buildings look weightless, emphasizing form and decoration.

There is no attempt here to fuse all the elements into one complex architectural composition. The buildings are placed on a large lawn like prisms on a baize cloth: the cylinder of the campanile, the box of the cathedral, the hemisphere and drum of the baptistry. They are not articulated into heavy and light, into shadow and high-light, but always as surface, and its decoration. The campanile's famous lean – somehow it leans too far to be quite credible – only adds to the impression that weight is not important here.

Pisa has the geological advantage of lying next to one of the world's great marble formations, and the unifying element of the whole cathedral complex is the beautiful white Carrara marble of which most of it is made. Subtle use is made of the deep-green and white banding, the zebra-work that was to become a dominant feature at Siena, Orvieto and also at Prato, from where much of the dark stone comes: *verde di Prato*. (The Orvieto stone is in fact grey basalt.) This banding seems entirely unclassical, although it may well be an exaggerated version of the Roman *opus mixtum*, in which courses of tufa stone were introduced at regular intervals within brick walling. It is entirely probable, however, that the Pisans picked up the idea from their trading ventures in the Levant, where this black and white work, Roman in inspiration or not, had been widely and very strikingly used for generations.

Apart from the refined work of marble-covered church and abbey, there is another, 'civil', Romanesque, where mass does come into play, where surfaces are less decorated, if at all. Much of this work has been demolished or remodelled in later centuries, but at Siena, San Gimignano, Lucca, Cortona, and Volterra there are substantial remains of public buildings or houses or both. The fortresses and castles of the period have largely disappeared, though Prato has one dating from the mid-13th century, rather behind the times in stylistic terms. This stylistic lag was inevitable in the smaller towns and villages, and well into the 14th century the Romanesque was being actively employed in the region.

Indeed the Romanesque was never wholly abandoned, and it informs quite strongly the **Gothic** architecture of the 13th and 14th centuries: the Pisan works of Santa Maria della Spina and the Campo Santo are two examples. Gothic architecture had been active for well over half a century in France before arriving with the Cistercians in Tuscany fully developed, at the abbey of Galgano, built between 1224 and 1288. The Cistercians were reformers, cutting back on the laxity and excesses of the Benedictines, and their architecture quite naturally showed a similar tendency towards austerity in decoration and simplicity of form. The characteristics of the Gothic are of course the pointed arch (an oriental form), light walling, and the supremacy of the vertical in composition. This did not altogether appeal to the Italians, and the Tuscans in particular cherished their love of decorated surface, even in their most purely Gothic works, such as Santa Maria Novella and Santa Croce, both in Florence. There is also a continuing interest in the balancing of height with breadth

– at least in Santa Maria Novella: that very classical characteristic that Romanesque and Gothic architecture struggled elsewhere to shed.

Galgano was built by French architects in the French Gothic manner. The church of San Francesco at Assisi, its contemporary, was built by Italians, and shows their interpretation of the style. Again there are the wide proportions, an almost complete absence of drama, balance and not vertigo. But a further point about Assisi: it is an architectural canvas, with large plain walls made to take frescoes; and so it leaves Romanesque, only to come back straight away to surface decoration.

Gothic detail was often applied, and very impressively, to otherwise largely Romanesque designs. There is a clear example of this in Pisa, where the 12th-century baptistry was Gothicized by Nicola Pisano around 1260. The Campo Santo at Pisa (1278–83) was built with Romanesque arches to the plan of a classical atrium, but later builders had no aesthetic problems about fitting traceried Gothic windows into those arches.

Siena, on the other hand, created in its Palazzo Pubblico, Campo, and many of the surrounding palazzi a great and substantial monument in pure Sienese Gothic, the most marked feature of which is the Sienese arch. Siena's Duomo offers a good example of a common occurrence, a building begun in one style and completed in another. It is difficult for us now to understand that the notion of a pure style in architecture is not much older than the 18th century.

There was a tendency throughout this late medieval period to produce an architecture whose aesthetic aims were to magnify scale and impress with sheer size, apparent in both ecclesiastic and civic building. In San Gimignano, city of towers, legislation forbade private citizens to build any that exceeded the 54m (180ft) of its own Palazzo Nuovo del Podestà. Similarly, before the Palazzo della Signoria in Siena was even begun, regulations were brought into force to ensure that all buildings facing the Campo would have windows of a uniform type, without balconies, and be limited in height. There is every probability that the whole development of the Campo, which had been a market outside the walls until the 13th century, was planned by the great medieval architect Arnolfo di Cambio.

What we may see as haphazard and unplanned was in fact carefully thought out and much debated. A growing interest in city planning is further illustrated by the appearance of cities in the frescoes of Cimabue, Giotto, Simone Martini, and others. Here was a medium where ideas could be easily tested in paint before being constructed in brick and stone: here we have the first essays in that love of theorizing that was to characterize every aspect of Renaissance culture.

In the early years of the 15th century, the Gothic bronze doors of Andrea Pisano were removed from pride of place on the east side of the Florentine baptistry. In their place were hung the new doors of Lorenzo Ghiberti, doors that sealed off a time as well as a space. Their sculpted compositions are rightly famous for the spirit of classicism that informs their conception and execution. But for all its seductive beauty, the coming age of classicism would be an end as much as a beginning. It was the end of the great experiments in style, the end of experimental and potentially democratic government, the end of artistic games where the rules could be understood by all. The Renaissance was, after late medieval times, a period of political and artistic tyranny. In its desire to harden the boundaries between social classes, to give fixed rules and correct models for artistic production, in its system of patronage and its promotion of universal order, it was perhaps a renaissance of the feudalism from which the people of the late Middle Ages had done so much to liberate themselves.

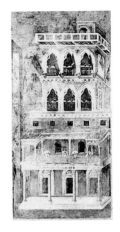

The Dream of the Palace. Detail of fresco by Giotto in San Francesco, Assisi.

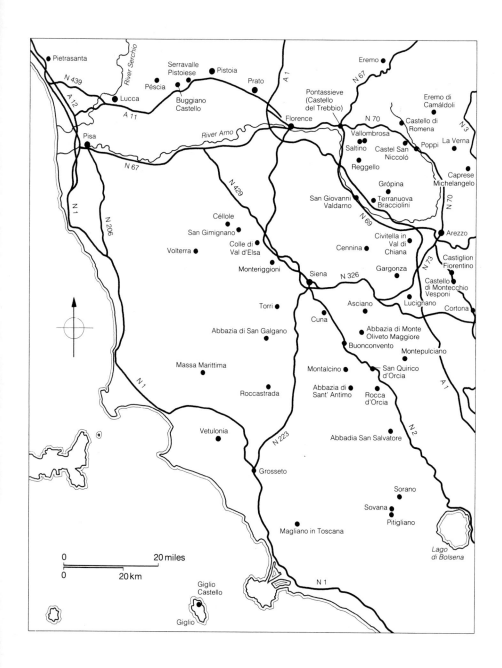

TUSCANY

During the thirty centuries of its history, Tuscany has remained very much the same cultural unit defined by its present regional boundaries. The Etruscan civilization, with its city-states, flourished here, and was a major influence on Roman artistic and cultural development. Even when conquered by Rome in the fourth and third centuries BC, Etruria formed a Roman region, the *Regio VII* of Augustus, that corresponds closely to the present territory. After the barbarian invasions it became a feudal unit, the Marquisate of Tuscany, with its capital at Lucca. During the centuries covered by this guide, that feudal dominion remained intact in principle, although for practical purposes it fragmented into a series of city-states, to some extent corresponding to the present provinces within the region. The stories of these city-states were outlined in the introduction; they are discussed more fully in the gazetteer section that follows here. The 16th century saw the region's gradual unification once more under the Medici dukes of Tuscany. It was eventually included in a unified Italy only in the last century.

The geography of eastern Tuscany is much the same as that of western Umbria. Hard soil means extreme annual cycles of wet and dry, and a vulnerability to flooding, to which the artistically disastrous flood of Florence in 1966 bears witness. North of the Arno are the Alpi Apuane, distinguished from the Apennines because they are a limestone formation; the river Serchio runs from them to the sea in a limestone basin, giving the land similar agricultural advantages to those enjoyed by eastern Umbria. The Alpi Apuane contain the great marble formations in and around Carrara. The greater part of Tuscany is taken up by hills lying outside the Apennine chain, divided from it by the valleys of the Arno, Chiana and Paglia rivers. In the west these hills are rich in minerals, the Colline Metallifere around Volterra.

(Opposite) Map of Tuscany.

25

THE NORTH
LUCCA, PISA, PISTOIA, PRATO

The road taken in the mid-sixth century by Alboin and his Lombard invaders when they spread from the Po Valley into Tuscany is now a good tarmac highway. But even today, as it crosses the Alpe Apuane at the Passo della Cisa, you get a hint, in the changing colours and softer contours of the landscape, that you are entering a wholly new territory.

The first town Alboin went for when he wanted to rule Tuscany was Lucca, and though he found smaller defences than the impressive 16th-century walls that exist today, the plan within them has remained largely unchanged since Roman times, and gates, streets and forum can still be clearly identified. The line of the Roman walls can be traced in the Via della Rossa and dell'Angelo on the east, Via Mordini and San Giorgio to the north, Via Galli Tassi, San Domenico and Cittadella to the west, and Corso Garibaldi to the south. But the **amphitheatre** is the biggest surprise, and provides a striking lesson about medieval town plans. For here is the amphitheatre all right, but the original has been 'dissolved' by time, and its place taken by later generations of buildings, in the same way a tree becomes petrified: the persistence of the plan.

Survival of street plans is no less important, but is usually less striking. The Franks of the Holy Roman Empire maintained Lucca's position as the first city of Tuscany. This was never a poor town, and the density of occupied buildings remained not far short of what it had been in Roman times. The landowners, artisans and merchants who lived here were, long before the millennium, busy building monuments with their surplus capital; above all they were building churches. Fifty-seven are recorded before 900, and although most of these would have been small they were evenly distributed throughout

LUCCA

(*Opposite*) Pisa: the east end of the Duomo, showing the apse.

27

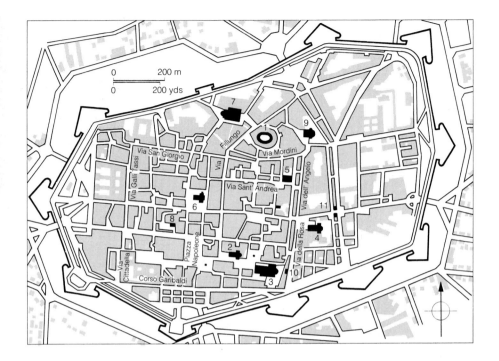

the city. But long before 1000 the city had outgrown its Roman walls, and in the tenth century about half the houses of Lucca were outside its gates.

This may seem to contradict the idea of an urban revival of the late Middle Ages. But essentially, Lucca – an exceptional city for its size and importance – survived as a Roman town. It was an administrative centre of Empire, home of landowners, and a consumer of rural produce. In these days it had not yet managed to pay its way with industry or commerce.

But with the rise of its silk manufacturing and banking industries in the 11th, 12th and 13th centuries the town became very wealthy. The *borghi* of Santa Maria Forisportam on the east and San Pietro Somaldi and San Frediano on the north grew in size and wealth, and in the 13th century were protected by a new line of walls.

* * *

Lucca has one of the most complex and interesting of

28

piazza groups in Tuscany. The Piazza Napoleone connects by the Via Duomo to the Piazza San Giovanni, itself connecting to the piazzas surrounding the cathedral itself: San Martino and Sant'Antelminelli. Piazza Napoleone does not concern us, and Piazza San Giovanni only partly.

San Giovanni is made up of two buildings, the church of Santa Reparata or San Pantaleone in front, and the baptistry dedicated to San Giovanni behind it. The church was built in the 12th century, and still has its original right flank and Gothic main entrance portal. The rest was refaced in 1622. The baptistry is a 14th-century rebuilding, a vast hall on a square plan, with pointed arcading on three sides and a high segmented dome. The older baptismal basin is hemispherical.

Lucca: detail of the San Martino group on the west porch of the Duomo.

Past the south side of the church to the east is Piazza San Martino. On the east is the **Duomo** with its tall campanile, to its right the 13th-century Casa dell'Opera del Duomo. The cathedral of San Martino was begun in 1063 by Bishop Anselmo (later Pope Alexander II) to replace an earlier structure. The asymmetrical façade consists of a great portico of three magnificent arches (the southernmost rather reduced by circumstances), above which stand three levels of open galleries, elaborately carved. A planned pediment was never executed, and it is a pity. One of the powerful columns supporting the main arches is carved with the 'genealogical tree' of Mary, and within the left-hand lunette is a carved *Deposition*, attributed to Nicola Pisano. Between the smaller right-hand and the central arches is the sculpture group of San Martino, 13th-century, as classical and serene as the front itself.

The upper part of the façade, built by Guidetto da Como (his name and the date '1204' are carved on the first arcade), is notable for the richness and variety of its decoration, in the liberal use of intarsia work and black and white contrasting marbles. Some columns are spiral, others smooth, some tessellated with coloured marbles, others carved: exemplary Pisan Romanesque.

The belfry was built later in the 13th century, a solid tower mimicking the tower-houses of the rich with its

29

Lucca: the west front
of the Duomo.

battlemented parapet. The cathedral's sides are later than
the front, and show Gothic windows between tall buttresses. Near the transept is a 14th-century statue of one of
the church's benefactors: fra' Fazio. But the most impressive part of the building after the façade, and perhaps the
oldest part of all, is the apse. The interior was rebuilt from
the late 14th century on.

  San Martino was a place of pilgrimage from the 11th
century, when it came into possession of the 'Volto

Santo', or Sacred Countenance, said to be a true likeness of Christ. The story is that after the ascension of Christ, Nicodemus was ordered by an angel to carve His image. Half-way through the task he fell asleep, but never mind: when he awoke he found the portrait completed by heavenly aid. This is the Volto Santo kept in the Duomo, brought out for display only three times a year.

San Martino occupies the centre-point of a cross-like group of piazzas, so that each side can be seen clearly, but the building can only at one point be seen from an angle.

Eastward, outside the line of the Roman walls, the church of **Santa Maria Forisportam** ('outside the gate') has a 13th-century apse and façade in Pisan Romanesque, though it was completed in the 16th century.

Back inside the walls, north along the Via Guinigi is Via Sant' Andrea, one of the most richly medieval areas of the city, where the **Case dei Guinigi**, a compact group of palazzi and towers of the 13th century, represent the last great flowering of the medieval tower-house. On Via Sant' Andrea stand the largest of the houses, built in the latter half of the 13th century, with its tall brick tower topped with Mediterranean oak trees. The ground floor has round-arched arcading on stone pilasters, while the two arcaded floors above enclose terracotta windows of three and four lights, Gothic in style.

On the corner in front of this palazzo stands a medieval loggia, now walled up, once used by the people of the *contrada* as a meeting place. In Via Guinigi (Nos. 22–4), opposite the palazzo's flank wall, is a second Palazzo Guinigi, 14th-century, with portico on the ground floor (now walled up) and three floors in brick with arches on pilasters and two- and three-light Gothic windows. Its tower has been knocked down.

At the other end of Via Sant'Andrea runs the **Via Fillungo**, one of the principal axes of the city, with several medieval houses and towers: the Torre delle Ore, 13th-century; opposite, another of the following century, and the houses identifiable by their brick and terracotta arcading and two-light Gothic windows.

From Via Fillungo, Via Santa Croce runs west into Piazza San Michele, the old Roman forum of Lucca, in medieval times turned into a market. The impressive Palazzo Pretorio is outside the scope of this book, but on the other side of the piazza stands the church of **San Michele**, a high-point in the development of the Pisan Romanesque. Begun around 1140, the work continued over the next two centuries. It is quite possible that the façade is the work of Guidetto da Como, who built the cathedral front. The same elaboration is evident, though here the work is carried to completion at the top, so that above the high arcaded ground floor, where the round columns are almost detached from the plain wall behind them, are four levels of arcading.

The plan is basilican, a plan borrowed from late Roman churches, and it seems that these arcaded façades may owe something to an attempt to compress, visually, the atrium that lay in front of the Roman buildings, into the space of a few feet. Actually useless as space, these 'narthex fronts' are sculptural memories of a working part of the early atrium-fronted churches.

Inside, the church is a basilica with nave and transepts divided by columns, and one or two Roman capitals can be seen among the medieval ones. The original open-truss wooden roof was replaced in the 15th century.

The building has a fine belfry, though its battlemented top was replaced in the 18th century. Around the church, particularly behind the apse in Via Santa Lucia and Chiasso Barletti, are several brick-built medieval houses.

North of the Roman city stands the church of **San Frediano** (St Frediano was an Irishman of the sixth century who became Bishop of Lucca), built between 1112 and 1147. This is a fascinating building. Before the erection of Lucca's new walls in the 13th century the church's orientation was reversed. The present façade contrasts strikingly with the two churches already discussed, although the plan of the church is again basilican. There is a sense of austerity, a Roman feel, purer than the later work because less elaborate in its detail, less enriched in its surface. The front is divided into three by pilasters (the outer bays left and right were added later to cover side chapels), its centre section running to nearly twice the height of the sides. Half-way up is a simple

Lucca: the west front of San Frediano.

loggia, not arched, above which is the splendid mosaic of the *Ascension*, protected by a dramatically projecting timber roof.

The inside is as austere in its architecture as the outside. Again we find classical capitals mixed with medieval. In the right aisle is the circular baptismal font (*fontana lustrale*) made around 1150 by Magister Robertus. Its base is decorated by two series of reliefs. The first series, by the same hand, is the story of Moses. The second tells the story of the Good Shepherd and the Apostles.

Other fine medieval buildings to see in Lucca are the churches of **Sant' Alessandro** (12th-century), **San Pietro Somaldi** (12th-century), **Santa Maria della Rosa** (façade *c.*1309), **Santa Giulia** and the remaining gate from the 13th-century walls, the **Porta di SS Gervasio e Protasio**, built around 1260.

PISA

For the Romans, Pisa was a port of considerable importance, and to an extent the city endured as an entity throughout Lombardic and Carolingian times by continuing its seafaring commerce. In 1004 the city was attacked and partly sacked by the Saracens, based in Sicily, but soon the Pisan navy was carrying out defensive and offensive naval operations against the Saracens off the Tyrrhenian coast, in Sicily, and even in Africa. The year 1015 saw the city forming an alliance with Genoa to drive the Mogahid and his followers from Sardinia, which was accomplished, but Genoa's jealousy at the territory falling under Pisa's control was ultimately to cause Pisa's downfall.

Her wealth continued to grow during the 11th century, with the Pisan navy helping the Normans with their invasion of Sicily in the mid-11th century, and transporting troops to the Holy Land during the second Crusade.

The following century was the time of Pisa's height. After Amalfi had exhausted herself in overcoming Muslim rivals from Spain, Pisa became one of the principal supports of the Empire in Italy. In 1162 Barbarossa granted the city vast territories, stretching on the coast from Portovenere as far south as Civitavecchia. Sardinia

Pisa

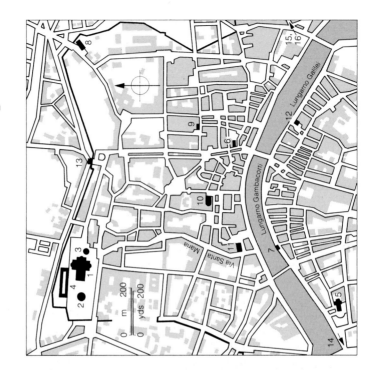

was granted her. But the greater Pisa's success, the hungrier the eyes that watched her. Lucca had warred with Pisa since at least the tenth century. Now, an alliance of Guelph states – Lucca, Florence and Genoa – determined to put down a common rival, and the decline of the Hohenstaufen dynasty in the 13th century only worsened Pisa's position.

The city defended itself well over a long period, but was decisively defeated on 6 August 1284, when the Genoese destroyed the greater part of the Pisan navy at the battle of Meloria. Civil war followed and the city's days of greatest power and wealth were over. The Florentines continued to pound away at the city, completely conquering it in 1406.

*   *   *

Pisan art underwent its major development during late

medieval times, never making significant contributions to the Renaissance. Three main cultures influenced the production of the Romanesque architecture that was to become identified with the city, and which was to have great influence throughout north and central Italy: the classical architecture of Rome, which could be seen in many surviving buildings; the Lombardic architecture that predominated before the millennium; and Muslim architecture, of which, with their expanding sea-trading empire, the Pisans had increasing experience from the 11th century. The new architecture made a remarkable first appearance in the city's **Duomo**, begun in the spring of 1064. A financial boost to the project came in the autumn of the same year, when the Pisan navy, their proposal to the Normans for a joint attack on Sicily having been rejected, attacked alone and captured six fully-laden

Pisa: the Baptistry, Duomo and Campanile from the west.

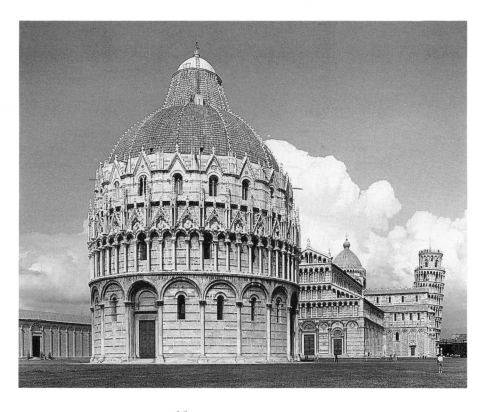

merchant ships at Palermo. One ship and its contents were sold and the money put towards the new building.

The church lies within its own large piazza, built on part of the Roman street plan, but outside the walls of the medieval town. The area had a degree of natural protection thanks to the swampy land surrounding it to the north, yet the site itself stood above flood level. The battlemented wall enclosing the piazza on the north is part of the late-12th-century city walls. Freeing themselves from the restrictions of a tightly-packed city, the builders had space here to amplify their ideas, and created the greatest masterpiece of Romanesque architecture in Italy.

Though incomplete, the building was consecrated by the pope in 1118. The original scheme foresaw a basilica plan of nave and four aisles, ending on the east with slightly projecting transepts, the whole plan a 'T'. But after 1087 it was decided to enlarge the project, bringing new aesthetic considerations into play. The nave was lengthened towards the west and the transepts were widened and raised in height by the addition of galleries over the aisles. This change forced the designer – or perhaps he welcomed the idea – to make the central dome elliptical rather than circular. All this seems to have been Buscheto's work. The apse and façade were designed by

Pisa: Duomo.

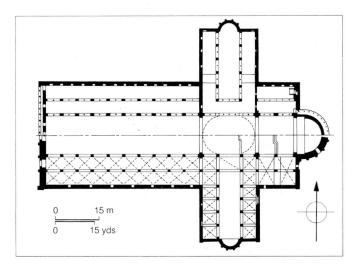

0   15 m

0   15 yds

Rainaldo, and the whole finished when the bronze western doors, by Bonanno Pisano, were fitted in 1179.

This one building manages successfully to integrate so many different stylistic elements that it became the prototypical Pisan Romanesque church. The façade arcading is essentially a Lombardic feature. The round-headed blind arcading below it, with its diagonally-placed squares as decoration, seem inspired by classical models; and the black-and-white zebra work of the nave, whatever its ultimate origins, must have come from Islamic sources. Interestingly, the triumphal arch that ends the nave is pointed and not round. The beautiful monolithic columns and capitals are antique.

Anxious that the Church should not get too grand an idea of itself from the flattery of such a magnificent building, the Pisans inscribed on its walls that it was built by and for 'the Pisan citizens, powerful in their renowned strength'.

Second in the series of monuments of the Duomo group is the **baptistry**, begun to the designs of Diotisalvi in 1153, again with a strongly classical feel, though the scheme also owes a great deal to the architecture of the Church of the Holy Sepulchre at Jerusalem, a building surely known to the Pisans through their involvement in the Crusades.

The building's first roof was the conical vault that still remains, though it had originally an open 'eye' at its top (as the Pantheon in Rome still does have). Externally a second row of arcading would have stood above the first, had the original plan been followed, and the outer wall would not have been so high. But Gothicizing changes were made beginning around 1260 with the work of Nicola Pisano, including the abandonment of the second row of arcading and the crowning of the first row with triangular pediments. Nicola's son Giovanni was at work on the interior after 1278.

It was some 80 years later, in 1359, that plans were made to put a dome on the building. To carry this new roof it was necessary to build up the outer wall of the baptistry – the conical vault rests on the inner circular wall – and this raised portion can be seen just above the round-headed windows with triangular pediments.

The interior of the Duomo at Pisa: the nave, looking east.

The Gothic works to this building, interesting as they may be from a decorative point of view, are little more than decoration, compromising the original conception of the building for no architectural advantage.

Internally the Romanesque space is largely intact, though with many Gothic details. In the centre of the floor is the octagonal baptismal font, by Guido Bigarelli da Como in 1246. It was the custom then to baptize adults *en masse*, on certain days of the year. Four smaller fonts for infants are built into the main basin.

To the left of the font stands a Gothic pulpit, hexagonal in plan, the work of Nicola Pisano and signed by him in 1260. Here is a work that for all its Gothic framework shows a remarkable tendency towards the plastic qualities of classical sculpture.

The **Leaning Tower** was begun in the August of 1173 to the designs of Bonanno Pisano, an example common enough in those times of a sculptor being invited to provide the plan of a major work of architecture. His idea was to mimic the Duomo's façade in a circular tower, but he evidently took insufficient account of the soft ground he was working on. It was taken up to the third storey before the work was stopped for a century, but in 1275 the work began once more under the direction of Giovanni di Simone. He tried to compensate somewhat for the earlier lean, and the result is a mildly curved cylinder. But it needed another century still for the work to be concluded, and the bells to be hung in their proper place. It seems that the tower falls out of vertical by an additional millimetre each year, so it cannot be long now before the *torre pendente* leans no more.

Giovanni di Simone also designed the cathedral's burial ground, the **Campo Santo**, begun in 1273 and mostly finished by 1310, though work carried on into the 15th century. This extraordinary building had its beginnings in the bringing to Pisa by Archbishop Ubaldo de'Lanfranchi of 43 shiploads of soil from the holy hill of Golgotha, in 1203.

He had this soil spread out next to the cathedral, apparently in a rectangular patch that matched the dimensions of Noah's Ark. Later in the century it was

decided to enclose this precious treasure, so that Giovanni di Simone's work can be seen as a rather special form of soil erosion prevention. The whole building is similar to a classical atrium, and it is remarkable how even this classical element has been detached from the other buildings and placed on its own. Internally the arches were filled with Gothic tracery as late as the 15th century.

In spite of the terrible bomb and fire damage suffered by this building in July 1944, the walls of the Campo Santo still hold a treasury of fresco work from the 14th and later centuries.

Pisa: the Campo Santo.

*   *   *

There is a good deal else to see in Pisa. **San Paolo in Ripa d'Arno**, in its homonymous piazza, is an 'urban church' dating from the 11th and 12th centuries, sharing the precision and control of the Duomo on a smaller scale. Badly bombed in 1943, it has been carefully restored.

The façade of the church of **San Michele in Borgo** shows Pisan Romanesque being dressed in Gothic clothes. It is the work of a certain Guglielmo in the 14th century, though the lower half is probably earlier. Here the three levels of arcading are given pointed arches and trilobed tracery.

Pisa: the church of
Santa Maria della
Spina.

But the treasure of Gothic architecture in Pisa is the little church of **Santa Maria della Spina**, sitting on the riverbank in the Lungarno Gambacorti. It was built as a type of reliquary to house a single thorn from Christ's crown. The building may originally have been an open loggia, but its present architectural form was created around 1323. It is revealing to see what an architect could do with Gothic when not restricted by the nave-and-aisles plan of most churches. At Santa Maria there is a richness of decoration more like French than Italian work, with the parapets erupting into a forest of spires, crockets and tabernacles. Yet underlying all the decoration is a rigorous geometrical scheme. The interior is a single space with a single roof, and its gable is prominent. But the two doors on the west front are given their own, lower gables, so that a rhythm is set up that both expresses the facts of the building and at the same time reduces the scale by breaking up the real unity of the space. In this case the general tendency in architecture, to make buildings seem more grand than they really are, has been reversed: a small building is intentionally made to seem smaller.

Other buildings worth seeing in Pisa are the churches of **San Zeno**, **Santa Cecilia**, **San Frediano**, **San Nicola** with its extraordinary belfry, and **San Sepolcro**, all dating from the 11th and 12th centuries. Outside the **Porta a Lucca**, a three-arched medieval city gate, a long stretch of 12th-century wall remains.

Not in but near Pisa are the churches of **San Piero a Grado**, west of Pisa and south of the Arno (11th-century); **Pieve di Calci**, east of Pisa and north of the Arno (11th-century); and the great **Certosa di Pisa**, east of the city and north of the Arno, dating from 1366 and after.

PISTOIA

The line of Pistoia's Roman walls can still be seen in Via Cavour, Via Pacini and elsewhere, and that of her medieval walls in Corso Gramsci and Corso San Fedi. The city's economy was agricultural but from an early time also industrial; in particular it produced iron weapons. The word 'pistol' is said to derive from the city's name, for this was one of the earliest and one of the largest centres of production of firearms in Europe. (I believe though that the etymology is false.) But it was the Pistoiese banking ventures in the 12th and 13th centuries that made the city briefly rich, rich enough to build a large number of beautiful churches and civic buildings, and rich enough to bring the Florentines to the walls to reduce the population to servitude.

The L-shaped Piazza del Duomo, on the site of the ancient forum, is here surrounded by medieval buildings: the Duomo itself, its belfry and baptistry, the Palazzo del Podestà, and the Palazzo del Comune. The **Duomo**, of the 12th and 13th centuries, replaces a fifth-century church on the same site. The façade shows a close relationship to its Pisan antecedents, but with less decoration and rendered more sober by the use of a darker building stone than Carrara marble. A further modification was made in the latter half of the 14th century when the distinctly Islamic-looking portico was added, with its zebra-work and stilted arches. Yet that portico's sloping pantiled roof, its windows and panels above the arches, and its higher central arch, all modify the oriental aspects in a classical way.

Pistoia: the west front of the Duomo.

At the north-west corner of the Duomo stands the impressive **belfry**, 67m (220ft) in height, whose lower half was built by the Lombards as a watch-tower. The three levels of arcading and green and white zebra-work walling were added in the 13th century.

More striped stonework appears at the **baptistry**, begun in 1338 by Cellino di Nese to the designs of Andrea Pisano and finished in 1359. The plan is octagonal – a common shape for baptismal buildings and fonts (as at Pisa) because the number eight is associated in medieval numerology with regeneration and rebirth. The main door has delicately carved capitals, while all three doors have been given very fine architectural decoration.

To the right of the baptistry stands the **Palazzo del Podestà**, or **Pretorio**, an austere building of about 1367. Within is an interesting courtyard and arcade, upon which are hung or painted the arms of the various men who occupied the post of Podestà over the years.

Opposite is the **Palazzo del Comune**, a massive sandstone building founded by the Guelph party in 1294, when the Podestà was a Florentine. Construction was interrupted by the return of the Ghibelline faction, but was taken up again in 1334; it was enlarged in 1348–53 and again in 1385. The ground level consists of an open arcade with slightly pointed arches. Above are three levels of windows, the first of double-light traceried windows, the

Pistoia: the Palazzo del Comune.

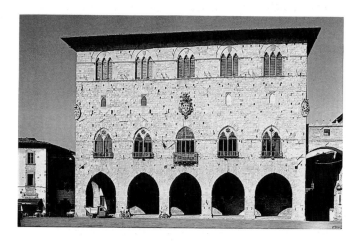

second of tiny rectangular openings, and the third of large three-light traceried windows.

South of the Piazza del Duomo is the church of **San Giovanni Fuorcivitas**, so called because when built it lay just outside the Roman city walls. On an eighth-century foundation, the present church was begun around 1250 and continued into the following century. The church is an oddity in that its main façade is its northern wall, even though its orientation remains regular, that is, altar at east. The situation seems to have arisen by default, since the west front is accessible. But that façade has never been completed. The architectural scope presented by this great flank wall has been well exploited. A 14-bay blind arcade runs the length of the building, above which are two further levels of arcading on a smaller scale. All the walling is striped with dark green and white marble. The details are crude but the effect of the whole is striking.

Other churches to see are **San Domenico** and **San Francesco** (13th- and 14th-century), **San Bartolomeo in Pantano** and **Sant' Andrea** (12th-century), and **San Paolo** (13th-century).

Prato would seem to have disappeared from history between the fall of the Roman empire and the ninth century, at which time the city was beginning to grow up around the church of Santo Stefano, now the Duomo. A commercial town, its political links were broadly with Florence, although its measure of autonomy can be gauged by the presence of the **Palazzo Pretorio**, built in two distinct phases. The older, 13th-century part is on the right as you look from the Piazza del Comune, and is made of brick. It was in fact a tower house, acquired for the commune's use by the Capitano del Popolo, Fresco dei Frescobaldi, in 1284. The open stairs, and the left-hand section in stone and its fine Gothic windows, were additions of the following century. The battlements were added in the 1500s.

The interior now houses the Galleria Comunale, with many important paintings from the 14th century and after. Many of the interiors retain their medieval character.

PRATO

Prato: the Palazzo Pretorio.

From the Piazza del Comune, Via Mazzoni leads north-east to the vast Piazza del Duomo, enlarged in 1293 after the *palazzi pubblici* there were destroyed during an insurrection.

The **Duomo** was founded in the tenth century and its rebuilding begun in 1211 by Guidetto da Como, who decorated the façade and side walls with blind arcading in the Pisan style. The flank wall is still visible. The 14th century saw the addition at the east end of transepts and chapels. The existing façade was built between 1385 and 1457, using the familiar dark green and white banding. This was built in front of the older façade, which still remains and can be seen from within the building. The external pulpit on the right-hand corner of the façade is a 15th-century work replacing an earlier Gothic construction.

Internally the addition of transepts and nave extension are integrated well with the older fabric, and give a culminating Gothic verticality to the more serene Romanesque west end.

From the Duomo, Via dei Tintori leads in an arc south to the **Castello dell'Imperatore**, or **Fortezza di Santa Barbara**, erected between 1237 and 1248 on the site of a fortified house by order of Frederick II. The building has a square plan and square towers at its angles, others rising

Prato: the Castello dell'Imperatore or Fortezza di Santa Barbara.

44

from its plain walls of white limestone. The battlements are made with the Ghibelline style of merlon – that is, swallowtail rather than square-topped battlements. The square-topped kind came to be identified with Guelph buildings. The castle interior was left unfinished at Frederick's death.

The church of **San Domenico**, 1283–1322, with late interventions by Giovanni Pisano, has an incomplete façade reminiscent of Santa Maria Novella in Florence.

Pietrasanta, on the N.1, north of Viareggio. The town's main monuments surround the Piazza del Duomo; among them are the **Duomo** itself, built 1256–58, enlarged 1330, later restored, and the church of **Sant'Agostino** (14th-century).

Serravalle Pistoiese, on the N.435. The town has substantial remains of medieval fortifications.

Buggiano Castello, north of the N.435, west of Montecatini. In the delightful Piazzetta della Pieve is the 12th-century **Palazzo Pretorio**, encrusted with armorial bearings, and the Romanesque **Pieve** itself, a Benedictine abbey church.

Péscia, north of the N.435. In Piazza Mazzini are the **Palazzo dei Vicari**, a large 13th- and 14th-century building, and the somewhat altered **Palazzo Comunale** of the early 13th century.

OTHER TOWNS AND ISOLATED BUILDINGS

FLORENCE AND ENVIRONS

Florence is in every way exceptional. Its site is not evidently much better than that of Pisa or Lucca, yet, powerful in both war and politics, it rose to become the dominant city of Tuscany in the later Middle Ages. While the other cities considered in this book reached their highest economic and artistic level during the 12th, 13th or 14th centuries and then went into decline, Florence continued to advance into the 15th and 16th centuries. Consequently, while Florence was often in the forefront of architectural enterprise during late medieval times, many of the buildings from those times were torn down and rebuilt in later centuries, whereas in most cities this could not be afforded. This is particularly true of the great family houses, like the Guinigi group in Lucca, almost all destroyed to make way for the new Renaissance palazzi, of which Florence offers a wealth of examples. Later still, in the 19th century, much more of what one might call the vernacular medieval fabric of Florence was destroyed when engineers carried out urban renewal projects, as they did in London and Paris, to 'ventilate' the city. (The Italian word for large-scale building clearance – *sventramento* – also means disembowelment.)

Florence was an Etruscan then a Roman city, but did not carry its importance through to the years of Lombard and Carolingian occupation. Little is known of the history of the city before the tenth century apart from the fact that it continued to grow after its sacking in the mid-sixth century, and that in the year 874 the bishop obtained temporal power over the inhabitants of his diocese. But by the year 1000, Florence was already among the largest and wealthiest of Tuscan cities. Over the next two centuries it built up a huge trade in wool with the north of Europe and in silks with the East, as well as an industry in money-lending that was to be second to none.

(*Opposite*) Santa Maria Novella, Florence. Detail showing the medieval lower part topped by Alberti's classical pediment.

47

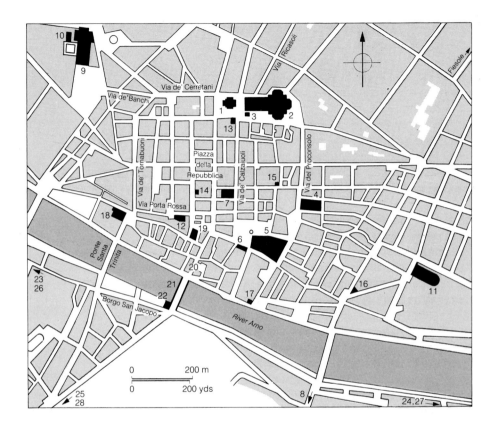

Florence
1. Baptistry
2. Duomo
3. Campanile
4. Palazzo del
   Podestà
   (Bargello)
5. Palazzo Vecchio
   (della Signoria)
6. Loggia della
   Signoria (dei
   Lanzi)
7. Orsanmichele
8. San Miniato al
   Monte
9. Santa Maria
   Novella

The establishment of trade markets involved continuous fighting, and the Florentines began waging war on their own account – rather than for pope or emperor – in the early part of the 12th century. This both demonstrated and reinforced the city's independence of external authority, and over the years the surrounding territory, or *contado*, was brought under the absolute control of Florence. Because the great landowning aristocracy, formed into the Società delle Torri, were also the military class, these men acquired considerable prestige and political power during the 12th-century wars. Such was the overbalance in their favour that their rivals, the merchants and the *popolo*, instituted the office of *podestà* in 1193. About this time began the renowned political rivalry that was to split the city into Guelphs and Ghibellines, a rivalry

popularly said to result from Buondelmonte dei Buondelmonti's jilting of his Amidei bride, and his subsequent
murder for this want of manners on the Ponte Vecchio, on
Easter Sunday of 1216. The struggle was in reality
between the Uberti family, who wanted a greater share of
power, and the commune. These local rivalries were
exploited by both papacy and empire, but the death of
Frederick II in 1250 left the Uberti and other Ghibellines
high and dry. They soon were expelled from the city and
sought refuge in Siena, where they sided with their city's
enemy and, in the fields of Montaperti a few miles from
Siena's walls, defeated the Guelph troops of Florence in
the early autumn of 1260.

It was not ten years before the Guelph cause had not
only won back their city but also defeated the Sienese,
their great rivals in banking. Although the names Guelph
and Ghibelline remained in use, their original meaning
disappeared with the Hohenstaufen emperors, and towards the end of the century a new duality appeared in
Florentine politics, with the Magnati – nobility and
landowners – in competition with the merchants and
artisans, banded together in the Arti. The Guelph party
now became official keepers of political orthodoxy,
banishing those suspected of 'Ghibellinism' and taking
their land and goods into their own treasury. It seems only
appropriate that the Palazzo della Parte Guelfa was taken
in this century by the Italian Fascist party for use as its
headquarters.

After the disasters of the mid-14th century, with the
giant Bardi and Peruzzi banks failing (largely through
unrepaid loans to the English monarchy), famine,
crushing taxation, and finally the devastating Black
Death, which carried off about half the population of
Tuscany between 1348 and 1350, Florence was headed
towards a government by *signoria*, which, while ostensibly
run on communal lines, would in fact be in the hands of a
single family. The deadlock between rival factions was
broken by the uprising of the Ciompi – wool carders – who
demanded their own Arte as well as a voice in government. This they obtained. But slowly the forces of
reaction forced them from power and sent their suppor-

ters into exile. It seemed that the league of merchants and landowners had triumphed. Yet it was the Medici family, who had supported the *popolo minuto*, the powerless lower classes, and who had gone into exile with their leaders, who were to triumph as dynastic rulers of Florence in the 15th century.

*   *   *

The years between 1150 and 1250 saw an immense growth in the size of Florence, whose population increased from about 15,000 to about 90,000 inhabitants. The monuments from this period that we see today were built against a background of ever-increasing density in housing, with tenement houses rising above shops along narrow streets, wood, brick and rubble buildings that were by and large unsafe and insanitary. These buildings had little to distinguish them from their neighbours, and formed a great grey sea against which the churches, especially those of the recently formed mendicant orders, stood out prominently. These large buildings were sited on the periphery of the town, where they had the space to make a fine architectural display, and on a scale in keeping with the expanding city. The older urban monuments, on the other hand, like the cathedral church of Santa Reparata, became scarcely distinguishable from the dense mass of building that enfolded them. What is more, the magnificent new cathedrals of Siena and Pisa, cities far less wealthy than Florence, made the old Florentine building look distinctly underwhelming.

A further difficulty in the way of Florence was the distribution of its monumental buildings in the city. Some cities have a system of linked piazze to connect their civic, market and possibly also religious centres, and manage to make something monumental from the combination. Others, like Pisa, had the space to develop one of these centres into an imposing building group. But the Florentine city plan shows each of these three functions isolated in the urban fabric, so that no scheme of design could unite these elements into an impressive display. Nor had they available free land to adopt the Pisan method.

Drawing of the unfinished medieval cathedral façade, made shortly before its destruction in the 16th century (Museo dell'Opera del Duomo, Florence).

In relation to the Roman walls, which were replaced in 1173, the cathedral was in the north-east corner, while the chief local market, the Mercato Vecchio, occupied the old Roman forum (the present Piazza della Repubblica) in the heart of town. The grain market was near the Mercato Vecchio, in the Piazza Orsanmichele, and near that again was the financial centre of the city, in what is now the Mercato Nuovo. When the Palazzo del Podestà was built in 1255, it was put on the south-east corner of that, just outside the line of the old wall. So here were religious, financial and civic functions as widely separated as they could well be in this city, and none had a building that could match the best buildings in rival cities. It seems very

likely that the three buildings I am going to discuss first –
the Duomo (and its accessories, the baptistry and belfry),
the market of Orsanmichele, and the Palazzo della
Signoria – were intended to form part of a new Florence,
whose great axial street on the line of the Via dei
Calzaiuoli would connect them all together: a new
Florence that was never fully realized.

THE
BAPTISTRY

The Baptistry of San Giovanni, standing to the west of the
Duomo, is in fact the oldest of the religious buildings
here, dating probably from Matilda's years, 1046–1115. It
stands on the foundations of a first-century classical
building that had the same octagonal plan form, perhaps
the Pretorium, and is built with a good deal of material
from that and other nearby ancient structures. The
cladding is deep green – *verde di Prato* – and white marble
in the usual Tuscan Romanesque way. About 1202 the
tribune was added on the west side, the so-called *scarsella*,
meaning purse or wallet, or a pilgrim's scrip. Between
1059 and 1128, while major works were being carried
out to Santa Reparata, the baptistry was the city's
cathedral.

In the 1320s it was decided to make bronze **doors** for the
baptistry. Andrea Pisano was sent to Pisa and Venice to
look at earlier examples of bronze doors, but technical
knowledge and artistic technique in the medium were
primitive. Andrea's solution involved dividing the doors
into 28 panels and assigning a different scene from the
Baptist's life to each panel. This was well within the
tradition of Giotto's fresco cycle at Santa Croce, and the
mosaic series within the baptistry itself (Venetian work-
manship to Florentine designs, of the early 14th century),
both illustrating the same theme. But the doors are doors,
with practical exigencies, and relief sculpture has neither
the colour of painting nor the stereotomy of sculpture.
The problems of making a set of doors into a work of art
should not be underestimated, and the solutions offered
by Andrea give us insights into the aesthetic sensibilities
of the time.

(Opposite) The
Baptistry and Duomo
of Florence from the
west.

He first broke the rectangular 'painter's field' of the 28 squares by framing each scene in a quatrefoil moulding, set on the diagonal. Looking ahead to Ghiberti's doors of the 1450s, it can be seen as one of that artist's main weaknesses that he failed to do the same. Andrea, within these frames, unifies the varied subjects of the panels by handling them in a similar way: these are mostly vertical-horizontal compositions, nudging their confines but not sweeping out of them. Technical aspects – such as the linenfold of the clothing – are as brilliant as anything in painting, and Giotto's painting at that. What Andrea achieves is a form in bronze relief that matches contemporary works in fresco and sculpture. His doors, incidentally, were originally hung opposite the entrance to the Duomo, on the eastern side, but were moved to make way for Ghiberti's second set of doors, made between 1425 and 1452. The northern doors are also Lorenzo Ghiberti's work, carried out between 1403 and 1424.

Entrance to the Campanile, Florence, showing Andrea Pisano's hexagonal bas-reliefs (see also page 14).

THE DUOMO

The present Duomo of Santa Maria del Fiore replaces the earlier cathedral of Santa Reparata, whose façade lay on the same line as that of the existing building, but which extended only a little over a quarter of its length. The sculptor Arnolfo di Cambio was in charge of the works when they began in September 1296, and his instructions were to make a magnificent building, the most beautiful building possible. He carried out the lower walls of his project and part of the façade, to a plan very like that of the present church, only smaller. There was to have been a dome. But Arnolfo died in 1310 and work slowed. Giotto, who took over his role in 1334, occupied himself mostly with the belfry, and died in 1337. When the work was taken up seriously once more in the 1350s, consideration of the design was in the hands of a committee that included painters and laymen, a reflexion of the city's awareness of its need for a large and prestigious building. By 1357 the design had been established and work was begun. Direction of the work was in the hands of Francesco Talenti and Giovanni di Lapo Ghini.

The building of this church allows us to glimpse

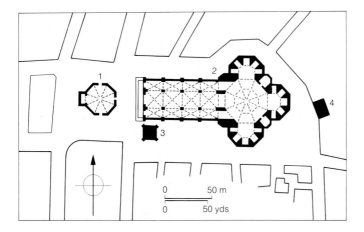

Florence: Duomo
1. Baptistry
2. Duomo
3. Campanile
4. Museo dell'Opera
   del Duomo

constructional processes that, unusual now, must have been common in medieval times. The old church of Santa Reparata was left standing while the new building was begun, as were the many houses east of the old church that would have to be demolished for the crossing and choir. We get an extraordinary picture of the high walls of this great cathedral rising among the tight-knit dwellings of Florence, some of which stood within the roofless building. Only when it was absolutely necessary were the old structures pulled down.

Yet although a design had been agreed and construction had begun, changes were still to be made. Artists were consulted, models made, the designs discussed, and even the general population of the city were invited to give their views. The plan under construction was to have been essentially a Latin cross type, the familiar Gothic plan. In the late 1360s the scheme for Santa Maria was altered so that the crossing would be, practically, three fourths of a centralized church, with the long nave running off on the fourth side. Over this would rise a dome, but not, as at Pisa, covering only the width of the nave: here it would cover nave and aisles too, and be the largest cupola built since classical times.

It is a measure of the Florentines' confidence that they went ahead with the fulfilment of this scheme without having the faintest idea how the great dome was to be constructed. The problem was solved in the 15th century by Brunelleschi, whose solution won a competition in 1420. The dome was closed in 1436, the lantern in 1461.

Internally the church shares the openness of many of the mendicant churches, with space flowing into the aisles unconstricted by the piers. The severe forms familiar from Arnolfo's other churches, as well as his interest in the expressive possibilities of planar surfaces (as at Santa Croce), are evident here, suggesting that the spirit of Arnolfo's architecture lived on through the changes made by others to his plan. The horizontality of the interior is equally evident on the outside of the cathedral, and a growing tendency to use 'passive' rather than 'active' forms can be seen in the use of round, rather than the Gothic pointed, windows to light the nave clerestory.

The nave is, for all its length, hardly large enough to hold the great dome. Yet the achievement is a compromise: while the nave is adequate to the church's use and the streets about it, the dome's scale is adapted to the city, and has come to both dominate and symbolize Florence.

Arnolfo's original façade – a sculptor's façade, full of niches and statues – was carried only a little above the main door in the 14th century, and stood like that until 1587, when to the dismay of many Florentines it was torn down to make way for a classical design. But this effort failed, and it was not until 1887 that the present façade was completed on neo-gothic lines.

THE BELFRY

The great belfry standing beside the cathedral, although planned and begun by Giotto in July of 1334, is only partly that artist's work. After his death it was carried on by Andrea Pisano, at whose death in 1348 it was taken up by Francesco Talenti and completed in 1359. Andrea is generally supposed to have been a victim of the Black Death, and it is interesting to see the Florentines, reeling under this and other disasters in mid-century, forge ahead with their city's great buildings as if nothing unusual were happening. This was just the time, as we shall see, that Siena was calling a halt to its own grandiose cathedral project.

Only the lower two 'floors' of the belfry, marked by cornice bands, are in fact by Giotto; the next two, divided vertically by pilasters, are by Andrea; and the next three above those by Talenti. The geometrical severity of Giotto's base gives way to the subtly divided pilaster bays of Andrea, and floridity finally breaks out above, as the tower pushes its way 85m (280ft) into the air. The use of coloured marble is especially pleasing: *bianco di Carrara*, *verde di Monte Ferrato* and *rosato di Maremma*. Bas-reliefs around the base are by Andrea and his followers.

Charles V apparently said that the belfry was of a rarity that should be covered up, and shown only occasionally.

From the east end of the Piazza del Duomo, Via del Proconsolo leads south to Piazza Santa Firenze and the earliest purpose-built civic building in the city, the Palazzo del Podestà, or Bargello, built 1255–60 and much added to and altered over the centuries. The oldest part of the building fronts Via del Proconsolo and Piazza Santa Firenze. The aesthetic qualities of the building are at the same time subtle and plain. The large Gothic window cutting through the second cornice, facing the piazza, was added in 1345 to light the Sala del Consiglio. The rear part of the building, facing Via della Vigna Vecchia and Via dell'Acqua, built 1352–4, follows the earlier design with minor variations. Inside is an impressive courtyard with an open stair (by Neri di Fioravante, 1345–67) leading up to the first-floor loggia.

PALAZZO DEL PODESTÀ (BARGELLO)

A second, grander building stands to the south-west of the Palazzo del Podestà: the Palazzo della Signoria or Palazzo Vecchio, built on the land where the houses and towers of the Uberti family had once stood. The Ghibelline Uberti had been expelled in 1258, and 40 years later the ruins of their houses still brooded in this corner of the city. The core of the Palazzo was begun in 1299 to house the Priore delle Arti, who at this moment of political upheaval could no longer safely remain in the house of the Cerchi family. These were the years of struggle between Black and White

PALAZZO DELLA SIGNORIA (VECCHIO)

Florence: the Palazzo della Signoria (Palazzo Vecchio) and its tower.

Guelphs written of by Dante, and indeed the years during which the poet was exiled.

Perhaps reflecting the urgency of the Priore's move, the core of the building was completed in the short span of years between 1299 and 1302, and the whole virtually completed in 1310. Tradition has Arnolfo di Cambio as the architect, and the quality of the work supports this claim. The original building is a great cubic block built of undressed *pietra forte*, divided into three levels by two thin cornices, upon which rest twin-light mullioned windows of marble. At the top of the wall, a projecting gallery circles the building, supported on arches and brackets. Beneath the arches are the nine arms of Florence. Round-headed windows puncture the gallery wall, which is crowned with battlements.

The tower, 94m (310ft) high, asymmetrical to the façade and dramatically thrust forward onto the projecting gallery, was built in 1310. Its base rests on the pre-existing Foraboschi tower, part of which can still be seen from within the palazzo. On top of the tower is a gallery similar to that of the main building but with ogee supporting arches, and its battlements are of swallowtail form. The lion and staff at the very top were put up in 1453, the clock made in 1667.

As civic display this is not sumptuous or luxurious, and while the building's fortress-like qualities probably derive from the atmosphere of civil war in which the project was conceived and executed, what the building displays above all is aesthetic control. The strict regularity and symmetry that were to become principles of Renaissance neo-classicism are not to be found here (the word symmetry itself, incidentally, in its original Greek form means 'visual balance'. It was another Renaissance trick to force a new meaning onto the word). But the wall itself becomes a surface of such cliff-like strength – a strength accentuated by the fractionally acute angle formed by its principal façades – that the variety of its door and window openings, far from seeming a weakness, becomes a humanizing element in the design.

The palazzo was enlarged under the Duke of Athens in 1343 (along Via della Ninna), and again in 1495. Inter-

Florence: the façade
of the Palazzo della
Signoria.

nally not much remains from medieval times other than
the Sala d'Armi on the ground floor. The lovely fountain
in the courtyard, for example, is a 15th-century replace-
ment of an earlier well. We are back to the main thesis of
this guide: most of the ideas are medieval even though
most of the actual objects are often not.

The building acquired its name as the Palazzo Vecchio
because Cosimo I de'Medici (1519–74) had it as his palace
before moving to the Palazzo Pitti in 1550. It was Cosimo
who, asserting his authority, had the words *Rex regum et
Dominus dominantium* carved over the main palazzo
door, replacing the earlier inscription, *Jesus Christus, Rex
Florentini Populi S.P. Decreto electus*, the meaning of
which was that there should be no ruler of Florence other
than Christ and the citizens.

Next to the Palazzo Vecchio on the south of the piazza
stands the **Loggia della Signoria** (also called **dei Lanzi**),
erected 1376–82 to the design of Benci di Cione and
Simone Talenti. This became the platform for the
Signoria's public ceremonies. The loggia is a characteristically Florentine interpretation of Gothic architecture with
its horizontal stress, semi-circular arches, and broad and
ample spaces. The result is really as much Romanesque in
style as Gothic.

**ORSAN-
MICHELE**

Florence: part of the
façade of
Orsanmichele.

The Piazza della Signoria corresponds roughly to the limits of the Uberti land and that of their fellow Ghibellines, the Foraboschi. From its north-west corner runs Via dei Calzaiuoli – the street of the stocking-makers, and the would-be grand axis connecting civic and religious quarters. To the west, along the Via Calimala and around the Mercato Nuovo, was the medieval business district, centre of a vast international trading empire but with nothing in the way of architecture to show for it. Opening onto Via Calzaiuoli itself is the piazza of Orsanmichele. Its name derives from the ancient church of San Michele in Orto (garden), demolished in 1229 and replaced in 1285 by an open loggia for selling corn.

The present building is something of a marriage of civic and religious functions, meeting each other as it were half-way along the street. It seems that the original loggia had become a pilgrimage shrine when a painting of the Virgin there began to work miracles. The original loggia burnt in 1304. In 1337 the commune decided to build a new loggia on a grand scale, completed 20 years later. This structure served as the corn market until the 1370s, when its arches were closed in and the building became a church. Yet at the same time two further storeys were added to the building, as a grain store. The chutes designed to carry grain from the upper floors to the ground can still be seen on pillars inside the church.

Even as a market this new loggia remained a place of pilgrimage, and its frescoes date from those days. This extraordinary melding of religious and secular functions seems also to have created a new architecture, where structure and surface are not merely decorated but are brought into active play in framing, supporting, and giving life to the works of art that are integrated into its fabric. The architect is unknown.

**SAN MINIATO,
SANTA CROCE,
SANTA MARIA
NOVELLA**

As we have seen at Orsanmichele, religious architecture had a substantial influence on – in a sense it saturated – secular architecture. This is not surprising. The church had every kind of head start on secular society. Disciplined, well supplied with intellectual talent and financial resources, and having as well a programme of religious worship that made specific demands on buildings, religious orders of all sorts made attractive models for civic enterprise. This places the religious buildings of Florence in a position of very high aesthetic importance, and although there are many churches of great interest in and around the city, I will discuss three of the most significant, lying in a triangle outside the 12th-century walls.

San Miniato, south of the Arno, became a model for much Romanesque architecture in Florence when it was

Florence: the façade of San Miniato al Monte.

Florence: San
Miniato al Monte.

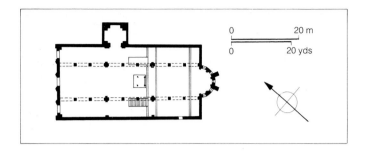

rebuilt after 1018 by the Benedictines, into whose possession it had come. The interior is a supreme example of an 11th-century basilica, restored in the 19th century but essentially intact. The plan has two aisles flanking a nave of three triple-arched bays. Column capitals are a mixture of antique and Romanesque. An open-vaulted crypt has meant a raised sanctuary, with access by shallow pitched stairs in each aisle. The roof is open timber trussing, painted in bright colours. The whole interior is alive with pattern and colour, every surface divided and subdivided by intarsia marble work, yet because of their simplicity the architectural forms read clearly through it all. There is a fine **pulpit**, and a beautiful carved marble **presbytery screen** of 1207.

The façade, later than the interior, has the same qualities. Five arches cross the lower level, three with door openings, the other two with 'door patterns' in marble. A straight cornice above supports a pediment across the whole front, with diamond-patterned black-on-white marble. But this pediment is interrupted in the centre by what is in effect a smaller temple front, standing on the cornice, with its own little pediment.

Santa Maria Novella lies to the west of the old centre of Florence, where the church's piazza opens off Via dei Banchi. This is a building for the mendicant Dominican order, hence the large piazza in front and the large and uncluttered interior space adapted to preaching. The plan is typical: nave and two aisles, short transepts and a square apse with minor chapels along the east wall. The nave is relatively low – relative to French Gothic – and the aisles comparatively tall. Each bay of the nave is matched by an aisle bay. Wall surfaces are plain, and the only variety comes from the use of the grey-green Tuscan *pietra serena* for the slim columns and arches – for the structural parts, in fact. This is as far as Italian Gothic was prepared to go in search of an architecture based on structural principles, and yet it keeps the wall surface in play – there is a tension between the two in this church that is the

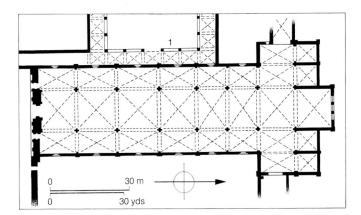

Florence:
Santa Maria Novella
1. Chiostro Verde

source of visual movement and overall aesthetic balance.

Santa Maria was founded in 1246 by Fra' Siso and Fra' Ristoro, though work on the nave seems not to have started until 1279, and the major building works were finished only in 1360. The façade was begun *c.* 1300, its white and green marble echoing the Baptistry and with similar Romanesque arches. In fact only the lower part, up to the cornice, was finished in the 14th century. A century later, Alberti added the top section, with its little temple front like San Miniato's but, unlike that church, having huge decorative volutes in place of triangular 'pediment' sections over the aisles.

To one side of the church is the **Chiostro Verde**, the green cloister, built in 1350 and so called because of the colour to which its beautiful 14th- and 15th-century frescoes have turned over the years. The old chapter house of the convent was put up by Jacopo Talenti in the

Florence: Santa Croce
1. Cappella Castellani
2. Cappella Baroncelli
3. Cappella Rinuccini
4. Cappella Bardi
5. Cappella Peruzzi

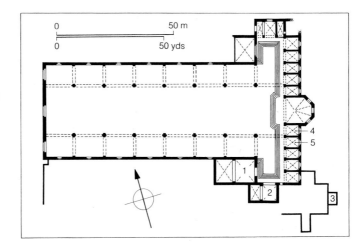

1350s, and is decorated with splendid frescoes by Andrea di Bonauito, *c.* 1355. Its present name, the **Cappellone degli Spagnuoli** (Chapel of the Spaniards), relates to its use by the court followers of Eleanor of Toledo, consort of Cosimo I, around 1540.

The church of **Santa Croce** lies on the other side of Florence, and its history exemplifies the rapid success and growth of the mendicant orders during the 13th century. St Francis himself set up a house here in 1211–12, and this was followed by the first church in 1225. Around 1252 this building was being enlarged or replaced, and by 1285 the even larger structure of the present church was being planned. Work was begun in 1294, and although the nave was not completed until about a hundred years later, there were no apparent changes to the design in that time. That the church was constructed at all aroused the fury of many Franciscans, who considered such luxury contrary to the spirit and principles of the Franciscan order.

The church is Arnolfo di Cambio's architectural masterpiece. Its plan resembles that of Santa Maria Novella but with five chapels instead of two on either side of the apse. This increase reflects the growing interest among wealthy Florentines in paying for chapels as family monuments, a practice that in fact helped finance the whole of the building operations.

This is not the sinuous northern Gothic, with its anthropomorphic and vegetal overtones. Santa Croce is prismatic. Nave and aisle roofs are not vaulted but use the open trusses of timber so common in Romanesque architecture, so that the nave becomes a triangular prism on top of a rectangular box. Although the nave walls are eaten away at floor level by vast airy openings into aisles, transepts and apse, the surface is maintained by a gallery-cornice running around all four walls below clerestory level, accented by a great climb up over the transept arches. The east wall itself, perfectly flat as it crosses into the transepts, with its great central arch and pediment, has the feel of a secondary façade, a church within a church.

The church gradually filled up with monuments and frescoed chapels, until in the 1560s Cosimo I initiated a 'restoration' programme, which included the removal of the monks' choir and the clearing away of many works of art. Heavy classical altars were added to the aisles. But some wonderful fresco work still remains. The **Cappella Castellani** has frescoes of 1385 by Agnolo Gaddi and pupils, the **Cappella Baroncelli**, frescoes of 1332–38 by Taddeo Gaddi (a pupil of Giotto).

The **Cappella Rinuccini** is an example of a nearly complete 14th-century chapel, with iron gates of 1371 and on the altar the polyptych by Giovanni del Biondo, *Madonna col Bambino e Santi*, in its original Gothic frame. The chapels on the eastern walls are more or less original in their architectural form, and the first two on the south of the apse (**Bardi** and **Peruzzi**) have frescoes by Giotto of about 1320. Plastered over or limewashed in the 18th century, these were uncovered and badly restored in the mid-19th century. Those in the Cappella Peruzzi were not really 'frescoes' at all, being painted onto dry plaster; not therefore so durable as fresco work, these have suffered badly.

It is something of a miracle that anything survives in this church. The flood waters of 1966 reached a level of 4.92m (16ft) in the cloister and caused enormous damage. In the church museum hangs the Cimabue *Crucifix* that was largely destroyed.

PALAZZO DAVANZATI

Florence: the Palazzo Davanzati.

A fascinating piece of domestic Gothic architecture is the Palazzo Davanzati in Via Porta Rossa, which conveniently happens also to be a museum, restored as a medieval house by Elia Volpi in 1906 and now in the hands of the Italian government. It was built for the Davizzi family about 1350, a tall building with three great doors in a ground floor of rusticated sandstone. Each of the next three floors has five round-headed windows. The open loggia on the top floor is a 16th-century addition and probably replaces earlier battlements. To the right an alley passes by the side of the house, which pinches in slightly on the ground floor, as does its neighbour, to make way. The façade retains the metal brackets and wooden poles resting between them in front of the upper level windows, which were used for hanging out the laundry, displaying fine fabrics, draping the curtains to keep out light while allowing ventilation, and hanging out caged songbirds.

The interior is rich with decoration and furniture. Of special interest are the courtyard, staircase – the lower part in stone, upper sections in wood – bedroom and kitchen.

OTHER BUILDINGS IN FLORENCE

Loggia del Bigallo, 1352–58, at the angle of Via del Campanile and Via Calzaiuoli.

Palazzo dell'Arte della Lana, built by one of the richest of the Arti, which in the 12th century had 20 factories, over 200 warehouses, and employed about 30,000 workers. The palazzo was built in 1308 and restored in 1905, since when the building has housed the Società Dantesca. The complex includes the battlemented house of the Compiobbiesi, and a smaller 16th-century building.

Case degli Alighieri, Via Dante Alighieri, in one of which the poet is said to have been born.

Loggia degli Alberti (Caffè delle Colonnine). Via dei Bentaccordi, which curves following the line of the old amphitheatre, leads to Piazza dei Peruzzi and then Borgo Santa Croce, where there is a tower-house of the 13th century and the Loggia degli Alberti, *c.* 1400, now occupied by the Caffè delle Colonnine.

Palazzo Castellani, Piazza dei Giudici, a three-storey house with round-headed windows.

Santa Trìnita, Piazza Santa Trìnita. One of Florence's most celebrated churches, built in the latter half of the 11th century by monks of the Vallombrose, it was enlarged and transformed into the present Gothic Egyptian cross ('T') plan in the latter half of the 14th century, perhaps by Neri di Fioravante. The façade is 16th-century, the interior a tripartite nave. Fragments of the Romanesque nave can be seen.

Palazzo dei Capitani di Parte Guelfa, Via delle Terme, begun in the early 1300s. The façade and courtyard, with covered external stair, are the early parts. Other buildings were added in the 15th century. Opposite are some 13th-century tower-houses, including that of the Buondelmonti.

Via di Por Santa Maria, 13th-century. Until the last war this was the most complete medieval part of Florence; it was almost wholly destroyed when the Germans blew up the buildings to block the approach to the Ponte Vecchio, the only one of the city's bridges they did not destroy during their retreat. Some tower-houses have been restored, including the Casa-torre degli Amidei, called also 'La Bigonciola', of the 13th century, the 14th-century Palazzo dei Carducci and the 11th-century Torre dei Donati Consorti.

Ponte Vecchio, built about 1345, architect Neri di Fioravante, and possibly Taddeo Gaddi. This was a bridging point in Roman times. The present three-light bridge was built after the great flood of 1333 destroyed its predecessor. Its width was sufficient to accommodate two covered arcades, in which the famous shops were built. Originally these were butcher's shops and the like, but since the end of the 16th century they have been reserved for jewellers. The timber extensions over the river are 17th-century additions. All the shops and the bridge itself were seriously damaged in the 1966 flood.

Above the left-hand arcades and shops runs the Corridoio built by Vasari in 1564 at the behest of Cosimo I, so that he could travel between the Pitti Palace, the Uffizi – formerly of course not a gallery but government offices – and the Palazzo Vecchio without using the streets. The corridor runs around the Mannelli tower at the end of the bridge, because the owner objected, not unreasonably, to its passing through.

Case dei Templari, at the southern end of the Ponte Vecchio, medieval houses. This is the beginning of the **Borgo San Jacopo**, a richly medieval quarter that suffered the same fate as Via Por Santa Maria but retains many fragments of medieval architecture.

Florence: detail of the massive doors of the Porta San Frediano.

Porta San Frediano, Viale L. Ariosto, built 1332 according to the design of Andrea Pisano. The gate is 8m (26ft) wide and has its original doors of timber and iron: 13.2m (43ft) high and 25cm (10in) thick, each leaf weighs 13,000kg (nearly 30,000lb), somewhat more than a fully-laden Harrier jump jet.

Porta a San Niccolò, 1324, complete apart from its battlements; part of the 14th-century walls, that circled Florence until the middle of the 19th century, large sections of which can still be seen south of the Arno. Also **Porta Romana**, 1326, to the south-west.

BUILDINGS
NEAR
FLORENCE

Badia di San Salvatore a Settimo, north of the N.67, south of the Arno, west of Florence. This is a walled church with tower, of 1371. It was given in 1236 by Gregory IX to the Cistercians of San Galgano, who had it until 1782. Damaged badly during the last war, it has since been restored. The façade is Romanesque-Gothic with a round 15th-century window. Good monastery ruins nearby.

Badia Fiesolana, east of the N.302, north-east of Florence. This site was developed as a monastery in 1026 and largely rebuilt in the 15th century by the Camaldolesi, who incorporated the old church façade within their scheme. That scheme was left unfinished at the death of Cosimo il Vecchio (1464). The old façade echoes the Florence Baptistry and the church of San Miniato al Monte.

Sant' Alessandro, Fiesole, east of the N.302, north-east of Florence. Built on the site of an Etruscan temple, this was originally a pre-Romanesque church of the eighth century, rebuilt in the 11th century, of basilica form, with nave and aisles. The glory of the building is its set of 16 magnificent columns of oriental *cipollino* marble, with Ionic bases and capitals, perhaps those from the temple of Bacchus, or more probably from the Roman basilica of the Forum.

Santa Caterina dell'Antella, Ponte a Ema, off the N.2, south of Florence. Built in 1387 by the Alberti family, the nave has Gothic arches and the whole interior is covered with frescoes of about 1387, by Spinello Aretino.

Santa Maria, L'Antella, off the N.2, south of Florence near Ponte a Ema. A large Romanesque church with an open-truss roof.

San Donnino, Villamagna, south of the Arno, east of Florence. One of the oldest parish churches in the vicinity of Florence, in existence since the eighth century; rebuilt in the 11th century in a severe Romanesque style. The interior has a nave (open-truss timber roof) and two aisles, with a semicircular apse.

Certosa del Galluzzo, west of the N.2, south of Florence. Begun in 1341 at the behest of Niccolò Acciaiuolo, the building has recently been largely restored to its 14th-century state and offers much to see.

THE WEST
SAN GIMIGNANO, VOLTERRA, MASSA MARÍTTIMA

San Gimignano delle belle torri e delle belle campane,
Gli uomini brutti, e le donne befane

Old saying

San Gimignano of the pretty towers,
Bells ringing pretty, sweet as flowers;
And men so ugly they make you start,
And women with looks to freeze your heart

San Gimignano, high on a hill and dominating the Val d'Elsa, lies at the heart of the Tuscan olive and vineyard country and conserves as few other cities its medieval character. It formed its commune in the 12th century, when it warred with its neighbours, most notably with Volterra to the south; a long period of violent civil war followed, waged between the leading families of Ardinghelli (Guelph) and Salvucci (Ghibelline). Its artists and builders were influenced by the Sienese, but as a Guelph city it usually sided politically with the Florentines. Yet the Florentines, dangerous enemies, were also risky friends, and in 1348 offered to take care of San Gimignano's political interests – an offer, needless to say, that was accepted. After this the town's political importance in the region was reduced practically to zero.

The city developed along the eighth-century Lombard road, the Via Francigena, as an agricultural market, and it is here that its principal buildings were put up in the 12th and 13th centuries. Fifteen of the family towers survive out of a number that in the 14th century reached 72. The quarters of San Matteo and San Giovanni grew up around the fortified centre and were enclosed in the second half of the 13th century by new walls, still largely extant.

The central market-place of San Gimignano was the **Piazza della Cisterna**, taking its name from the well, built

SAN GIMIGNANO

(*Opposite*) San Gimignano: the rear courtyard of the Palazzo del Popolo.

71

in 1273 and enlarged in 1346, that stands within it. Triangular in plan, the piazza is surrounded by medieval houses and towers. On the south side, beginning with the Arco dei Becci on the right, is a fine series of buildings. The Casa Razzi is in fact a house in two parts, with normal living quarters on the right and, on the left, with its own separate door, a defensive tower. Casa Salvestrini follows, dating from the 1200s, formerly the Ospedale degli Innocenti and now the Cisterna Hotel. The Palazzo Tortoli with two orders of twin-light windows is of the Sienese type of the 14th century, and beside it is the fragmentary tower of the former Palazzo del Capitano del Popolo.

On the north side, starting from the Via del Castello, is the Palazzo dei Cortesi, with the high *Torre del Diavolo* (Devil's tower). The west side includes the Casa Semplici and the Casa Magazzini, as well as the impressive twin 13th-century towers of the Ardinghelli.

Joining this piazza at its north-west corner is the trapezoidal **Piazza del Duomo**, completed in its present form at the end of the 13th century and serving as both the civic and the religious centre of the city. The **Palazzo del Podestà** was rebuilt in 1239 and enlarged in 1337; it has a façade partly stone and partly terracotta. An arched loggia at ground level leads to the great *Torre Rognosa* ('scabby tower'). Left of the Palazzo del Podestà is the Torre Chigi, built in 1280. To the north are the two towers of the Salvucci family.

The west side of the piazza is dominated by the Collegiata or **Duomo**, which is not, as you might expect, dedicated to San Gimignano, but to Santa Maria Assunta. Gimignano is the patron saint of Modena, and that is where his bones are. Santa Maria, consecrated in 1148, is a good 12th-century Romanesque design. There are wonderful frescoes illustrating the New Testament, by Barna da Siena, of the mid-14th century, and the Old Testament, by Bartolo di Fredi, about 1367.

The southern side of the Piazza del Duomo is taken up by the **Palazzo del Popolo**, also called the Palazzo Nuovo del Podestà, completed in 1288 and enlarged in 1323. On the right is a balcony at the top of a staircase, the *arengo*, from which politicians would harangue the crowd of

citizenry, and also on the right, the tallest of San Gimignano's towers, at 54m (177ft), the **Torre Grossa**. The building is now the city museum. In the Sala di Dante (in 1300 the poet argued here the necessity for a Guelph league in Tuscany) is a large fresco *Maestà*. This is a reworking of Simone Martini's more famous painting in Siena of a few years earlier, done by Lippo Memmi and dated 1317. Other frescoes in the room are of the 13th and 14th centuries. The view from the tower is splendid.

General view of San Gimignano.

Via San Matteo, running north from the Piazza del Duomo, with its travertine paving and flanked by medieval palazzi, is the city's most picturesque street. No.2 on the right, opposite the Salvucci towers, is the palazzo and tower of the Pettini family. Next is a double arch in stone, the Arco della Cancelleria, an ancient gate from the city's first circle of walls. A series of medieval houses follows: Palazzo della Cancelleria (chancellery) of the late 1200s; the 13th-century Romanesque church of San Bartolo, with its façade of terracotta and brick and blind arcading on the upper levels, on the Pisan model; the tower-house of the Pesciolini (No.32), Florentine style of the late 1200s; farther up, at No.60–2, the two buildings that make up the Palazzo Tinacci. The street is closed on the north by the Porta di San Matteo, built in 1262 in Sienese style.

From the Porta San Matteo, Via Cellolese leads to the Piazza Sant' Agostino, with, on the left, the 11th-century Romanesque church of **San Pietro**. The inside has only a nave and no aisles, all very rustic, with a wooden roof and votive frescoes of the 14th-century Sienese school.

Sant' Agostino, a Romanesque-Gothic construction of 1280–98, has a plain façade and is full of beautiful fresco work, all of it outside our period except for one on the left wall by Lippo Memmi of around 1330.

To the east of the town is the Porta and the Romanesque church of **San Jacopo**, founded, according to tradition, by the Templars in the 13th century. The façade is in brick and stone, with two doors of the Pisan type, and above them a rose window. Sienese majolica plates of the 13th century decorate the terracotta cornice. Inside is a single nave with Gothic arches.

A road south here runs outside the medieval walls of 1262 and leads to the **Porta alle Fonti**, so called because of the nearby fountains used for washing sheep's wool, a structure of ten arches built at various times between the 12th and 14th centuries.

On the south of Piazza della Cisterna, through the Arco dei Becci (part of the original walls) and to the east, are the Torre dei Becci, in Via degli Innocenti. Via San Giovanni leads south to the Piazzetta dei Cugnanesi with its immensely tall tower, belonging to the Palazzo Cugnanesi of the 13th century. The finest building in Via San Giovanni is the **Palazzo Pratellesi**, stone and brick, 14th-century, with twin-light Gothic windows. The finest gate in the city, **Porta San Giovanni**, is at the end of the street, again of 1262 and Sienese in style, with a guard-room above.

A few miles, through olive groves and vineyards, to the north-west of San Gimignano, the parish church of **Céllole** stands shaded in a cypress grove. Built of travertine in the Romanesque style and consecrated in 1237, it has a broad, plain façade, with a central door. The interior, with a nave and two aisles, has fine columns and capitals, a timber roof, and a lovely semicircular apse, decorated by a band of carved arcading. The octagonal baptismal font is carved from a single piece of travertine.

VOLTERRA

The city of Volterra stands 550m (1800ft) above sea-level, on the watershed between the two river basins of the Val

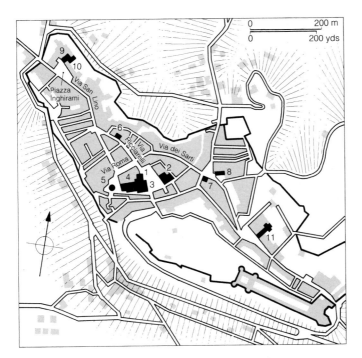

Volterra
1. Piazza dei Priori
2. Palazzo Pretorio
3. Palazzo dei Priori
4. Duomo
5. Baptistry
6. Casa Ricciarelli
7. Torre Toscano
8. San Michele Arcangelo
9. San Francesco
10. Cappella Guidi
11. Sant'Agostino

dell'Era to the north and the Val di Cècina to the south, commanding, beyond olive groves in the foreground, a magnificent view of both mountains and sea. This is an ancient city, and was a powerful centre in Etruscan times. In fàct the Etruscan walls, most of which still exist, at over 7km (nearly 5m) in length are of a far greater extent than the medieval city walls. A bishopric from the fifth century, Volterra was an important administrative centre for the Church. The commune organized early here, rebelling against the hereditary rule of the Pannocchieschi family (1150–1239).

The city, like all the others at this time, was now Guelph, now Ghibelline, forming opportunistic alliances and fighting wars with Florence, Pisa, San Gimignano and Siena, until in 1340 it passed into the hands first of the Belforti and then of the Florentines, who took control definitively from 1361. Subsequent attempts to shake off this outside domination continued during the 15th and 16th centuries. The economy was based most obviously on agriculture, but also on the working of alabaster, which is found in quarries throughout the region. The little alabaster Leaning Towers you buy in Pisa are made here.

The medieval city is circled by walls that were built by order of Emperor Otto I in the tenth century. They and most of the buildings within them are constructed in the dark grey shelly limestone local to the area.

The heart of Volterra is **Piazza dei Priori**, certainly among the most strikingly beautiful of medieval Italian piazze. The tall grey palazzi that surround the space, mostly medieval but some in imitation, give an impression whose severity embodies the popular notion of the Middle Ages. On the south-east side is the Palazzo Monte Pio, restored this century, and adjoining it on the north-east side the **Palazzo Pretorio**, an agglomeration of 13th-century buildings and formerly residence of the Capitano del Popolo. From the tower on the right of the Palazzo Pretorio hangs the ill-defined figure of an animal, popularly known, like the tower itself, as 'the Piglet'. On the north-east side is the Palazzo Incontri, now a bank and largely restored, and on the south-west the bishop's palace, built as a public granary and given its present use only in the late 15th century.

Volterra: the Palazzo dei Priori.

But the **Palazzo dei Priori** is the building that dominates this piazza, the oldest communal building in Tuscany, built between 1208 and 1254. The façade is divided into three levels with plain cornices. The lowest level, with one great door and three small windows, is decorated with the arms of the various Florentine representatives who ruled here. The level above is more ordered, with a series of four Gothic windows on the left and a single similar window on the right. Above, the pattern is repeated, with fewer windows but always with the gap on the right-hand side. This stretch of plain wall makes you look up: straight above is a battlemented tower (second level added in 1846). The notion of the wall was so ingrained into the medieval psyche that it was instinctively understood, and handled with marvellous subtlety. The northern Europeans, with their Gothic and then neo-classical, have always tended towards the columns: forest dwellers. But even in the Renaissance the Italians retained their love of walls, and as late as the 18th century Piranesi fought a rearguard action against the intrusion of Greek – columnar – architecture. The Palazzo now houses the city's art gallery, the Galleria Pittorica. The tower deserves a visit for the splendid view of the Alpe Apuane to the north, the Colline Metalliferi to the south, and to the west the sea.

Left of the Palazzo dei Priori the Via Giusto Turazza runs past the side of the **Duomo** and leads into the Piazza San Giovanni with the baptistry straight ahead. The cathedral is 12th-century Romanesque, reworked in the following century to bring it in line with Pisan standards. The façade is organized on two levels, separated by a cornice. The lower level has robust pilasters on the angles and a projecting centrepiece, into which have been carved the main door and two blind arches beside it. The door surround is in marble with geometrical mosaic in the arch above it. Above the cornice are a large rose window and a pediment of blind arcading.

Internally the building was redone during and after the Renaissance, but in the second chapel of the right transept is one of the great works of Romanesque sculpture, a wooden *Deposition* group dating from the mid-13th century.

Facing the Duomo is the octagonal **Baptistry**, constructed in the 13th century and presumably at the same time that the cathedral was being altered. There is something peculiar about this free-standing building with its one side – the face that looks across the piazza at the cathedral – decorated with striped black and white marble, the rest made of Volterra's grey limestone. The apparent lack of ambition combined with a desire to impress somehow disappoints.

North of the Piazza San Giovanni, Via Roma enters Via Ricciarelli at a point known as the 'crossing of the Buonparenti', perhaps the most characteristically medieval section of Volterra, mostly of the 13th century. It includes the **Casa Ricciarelli**, the tower-house of the Buonparenti, and tower-houses of various other families: Martinoli, Nannetti and Miranceli, and Buonaguidi. Farther east in Piazzetta San Michele are the **Torre Toscano**, made up of a 13th-century tower of rusticated

Volterra: medieval houses near the Via Buonparenti.

stone, and an ashlar house of the following century. The little Pisan Romanesque church of **San Michele Arcangelo** shares this piazzetta.

To the north-west, in Piazza Inghirami near the limits of the medieval city, is the 13th-century church of **San Francesco**, of which little original remains. But beside it is the wonderful **Cappella Guidi** or **della Croce di Giorno**, built in 1315 and entirely covered in frescoes in 1410. The evangelist figures on the ceiling of the first section of the chapel are the work of Jacopo da Firenze, and the rest are by Cenni di Francesco Cenni, illustrating the legend of Santa Croce (inspired by Agnolo Gaddi's frescoes at Santa Croce in Florence) and many others.

MASSA MARÍTTIMA

Massa Maríttima is another city like Volterra, Etruscan in origin, of little significance in Roman times, and given importance in the Middle Ages by the Church. In the ninth century the bishopric was transferred to Massa from the ancient Populonia. Sacked by the Saracens in 935, the town later thrived on the mining of local copper and silver deposits. Naturally there were the usual wars and alliances with Pisa and Siena, with the latter finally incorporating

Massa Maríttima: view west over the Città Vecchia from the Città Nuova.

the commune into its own territory in 1335. When Siena fell to the Florentines Massa went with it, and from the 16th century its decline was steady. Mining stopped completely in 1396. The position was aggravated by endemic malaria that plagued the city until well into the 19th century, when the encroachment of swampland nearby that had been progressing for five hundred years was reversed by land drainage schemes.

The city is divided into two distinct parts, the lower Città Vecchia, where Romanesque architecture prevails, and the Città Nuova at a higher level, largely Gothic. The two 'cities' are connected by a single steep road.

At the heart of the Città Vecchia is the striking Piazza Garibaldi, with its **Duomo** that seems quite out of scale to a town of this size, of fine honey-coloured stone. It was begun along Pisan models in the early 1200s, subsequently modified on the east end, still holding with the Pisan exemplars, in 1287 and 1304. The lower level of the façade has seven round-headed arches, decorated with diamond patterns, and above are two levels of blind arcading. The building is seen from the left, and whether intentionally or not, a slight diminishing of the intercolumniation on the right-hand columns exaggerates the perspective effect.

Massa Maríttima
1. Duomo
2. Palazzo Pretorio
3. Palazzo Comunale
4. Palazzo dell'Abbondanza
5. Fortezza dei Senesi
6. Sant'Agostino

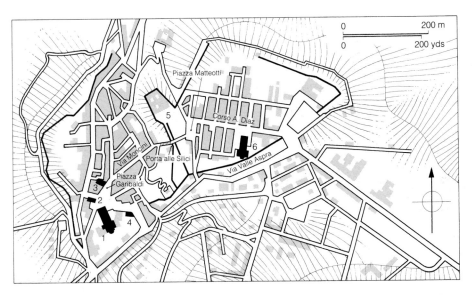

79

The campanile, with its multiplying openings on progressive levels, was rebuilt early in this century to the original design.

Inside there is some good stained glass from the 14th century in the rose window. In the southern aisle is the old baptismal font, a rectangle of about 275 × 245cm (9 × 8ft) and over 90cm (3ft) tall, carved out of a single block of travertine. The lovely reliefs around its sides are the work of Giroldo da Como, working around 1267.

On the altar of the Cappella della Madonna, in the north transept, is the damaged *Madonna delle Grazie*, painted by the Sienese artist Duccio di Buoninsegna or one of his pupils around 1316.

From a door to the left of the main altar a stair descends to a pair of underground rooms, the Cappella delle Reliquie, and the Soccorpo. In the latter stands the *Arca di San Cerbone*, an important work of Sienese sculpture, signed by Goro di Gregorio and dated 1324. It is said to be carved of marble but it looks soft, more like alabaster, and the carving work would seem to bear this out: although the figures are so severely undercut as almost to detach themselves from the panels they are carved from, there is little sharpness of detail. Traces of colour indicate that the whole thing was originally painted.

Opposite the Duomo is the **Palazzo Pretorio**, ancient residence of the Podestà, a massive structure on three floors built in 1230. To its right is the fine Casa dei Conti di Biserno, 13th-century Romanesque with later alterations, and adjoining this the **Palazzo Comunale**, a grand complex of medieval buildings dating from the early 13th to mid-14th centuries. The palazzo was in fact formed by uniting three pre-existing tower-houses. The left-hand section, originally lower, dates from the 1340s; the central part was built slightly earlier in the same century by the Sienese Stefano di Meo and Gualtiero di Sozzo; and the right-hand section, called the Bargello, was put up in the early 1200s.

Behind the Duomo is the fascinating **Palazzo** or **Magazzino dell'Abbondanza**, built in 1265 following Sienese models. It consists of three massive pointed arches and a vaulted space beyond which is the public fountain. Above this is built the granary of the Sienese administration – hence the building's name.

Via Moncini leads east and to the Città Nuova, climbing a steep ramp and passing through the 14th-century Porta alle Silici that separates the two cities, before opening out into Piazza Matteotti. The plan of this town – which after all is 13th- and 14th-century – is significantly a rectilinear street plan. In the piazza stands a remnant of the fortress built by the citizens in 1228, the Torre del Candeliere or dell'Orologio. That fortress was subsequently linked to the much more massive **Fortezza dei Senesi** by means of a beautiful stone bridge. The apparent lightness of this structure is exaggerated by the massive buildings it links together. There are substantial remains of the Sienese fortress, though it has been picked away at over the years to make way for the local hospital.

Farther east, half-way along Corso Diaz, is the Romanesque-Gothic church of **Sant'Agostino**, also confusingly known as San Piero all'Orto, from an earlier church on the site. The present church was built between 1299 and 1313. The façade is plain and bare travertine, with a large door and rose window above. The splendour of the church is its interior, a single nave of six arches, crude, heavy, and immensely powerful. This is beauty raw and not refined.

Colle di Val d'Elsa, at the junction of the N.541, N.68 and N.2. There are two towns here, and it is the Colle Alta that interests us, though the lower town, il Piano, does offer us the **Badia di Spugna** – Sponge Abbey – which you may think should be a novel by Thomas Love Peacock, or one of the Brontës, but is in fact a tenth-century building, now a farm. The town is the birthplace of both Arnolfo di Cambio and Cennino Cennini. Its prosperity in medieval times was founded on paper-making and wool manufacture.

The Colle Alta has most of its 12th-century walls intact as well as a fine tenth-century castle and a number of medieval houses, in the Via Gracco del Secco, Via dell'Amore and particularly in Via del Castello, where at

OTHER TOWNS AND ISOLATED BUILDINGS

No.63 is the tower-house of Arnolfo di Cambio, of the early 13th century. **Via delle Volte** is a street that passes under vaulting for about 100m (330ft), suggestive of the close density to which these towns were built in medieval times.

Monteriggioni, off the N.2, north of Siena: a small and picturesque town founded in 1203 by the Sienese as an outpost against the Florentines and passed frequently from one city to the other. Its walls, guarded by 14 towers, were raised in 1213–19 and reinforced in 1260–70, with a circumference of 570m (625yds). The town within still preserves its medieval atmosphere.

Torri, south of the N.73. This is a small town that still has much of the medieval about it, in its houses and small buildings. Nearby is the **Abbazia di Torri**, a Vallombrosian monastery of the later 13th century, with a lovely cloister, square in plan and surrounded by a three-storey arcade: lowest level of black and white marble, on various shapes of column; middle on terracotta pilasters; upper on small wooden columns.

A medieval street in Torri.

Detail of a window in the Abbazia di San Galgano.

Abbazia di San Galgano, off the N.441. This is the most important Cistercian building in Italy after the abbey at Fossanova, farther to the south in the region of Lazio. Mostly now ruined, and standing alone in the countryside, the Latin-cross church was built according to French Cistercian principles between 1224 and 1288, of brick and travertine, and had immense importance in the diffusion of Gothic architecture in Tuscany. The scheme should be familiar to the English: solid and well-proportioned pointed arches dividing the tall nave from the aisles, rose window in apse and transepts – all very austere. Other parts of the monastery can be seen: chapter house, cloister, cells.

By the 13th century this monastery was the biggest landowner for miles about, having supplanted and dispossessed a large number of Benedictine institutions. Its monks were often chosen by the commune of Siena, the bishops of Volterra and private citizens to arbitrate disputes, and were judges, lawyers, doctors, architects and building workers at the Duomo in Siena. But in the late 13th century it was devastated on more than one occasion by Giovanni Acuto, and in the years following it went ever farther into decay. After 1816 the buildings were used as a farm, but now part of it has been restored for use as an Olivetan monastery.

Of great interest and delight is the nearby **Chiesetta di San Galgano**, a circular Romanesque building with a roof of tile and travertine in concentric rings. An adjacent chapel is filled with frescoes by Ambrogio Lorenzetti.

Detail of the roof interior at the Chiesetta di San Galgano.

Roccastrada, on the N.73: 13th- and 14th-century town.

Vetulonia, off the N.1 near the junction with the N.73 (near Grosseto): a town whose medieval fabric survives.

Grosseto. Only the **Duomo** survives here from medieval times, built 1294–1302 by Sozzo di Rustichino on the remains of an earlier Romanesque church, though it was refaced in the 19th century. Narrow bands of red marble, *rosso di Caldana*, alternate with broader bands of white marble. There are three doors on the lower level and an open arcade running up the aisle roofs and across the nave façade above. Higher up is a large rose window. The interior was remade in the 16th century.

Magliano in Toscana, on the N.323 (near Orbetello). The church of San Giovanni Battista is originally Romanesque, with subsequent alterations. Nearby is the ruined church of San Bruzio, Lombardic Romanesque begun around the year 1000, finished about 200 years later: a grand ruin.

Giglio Castello, Isola del Giglio (Orbetello). You must get the boat for this one, and spend a quiet time on the lovely island of Giglio. Giglio Castello is perched on a high precipice, its medieval walls and towers complete, or nearly so. The town is full of narrow and tortuous streets, labyrinthine lanes with arches overhead, steep stairs.

THE SOUTH
SIENA AND SOUTH

You may well wonder why Siena ever became a city at all.
It does not have a naturally gifted location like Florence
or Pisa; it is not on a river and does not dominate any river
valley; nor is it a naturally well-fortified place, particularly
on the north – the Florentine – side. It was the Romans,
with their sense of pragmatism, who made Siena a city.
For them a city was not, as it was later to develop in the
Middle Ages, an economic unit, but an administrative
centre. A Roman city had its territory to administer and it
survived by taxing that territory. To a certain extent this
was true of the medieval city as well; the city and its
contado were one administrative and economic unit, and
only gradually did the city's specialization develop suf-
ficiently to enable it to have a truly independent existence.

It may be said that Siena never made this step into the
modern world, and that its existence today as the largest
'medieval' city in Europe bears witness to that fact. We
have seen that Florence, in spite of its great development
in medieval times, continued its progress in the Renaissance period, losing some of its ancient character and
buildings, certainly, but staying alive economically. Siena
did not, and the banking industry which it had founded in
Italy was snatched from its hands by the Florentines. The
city we admire today, with its remarkably uniform texture
of 13th- and 14th-century buildings, is a physical survival
of something that died economically.

As a bishopric, Siena was early enmeshed in medieval
politics, and soon was reasserting its 'Roman' rights over
the surrounding countryside, knocking down castles and
arrogating the rights of local feudal lords. Its rivalry with
Florence was an early development, and the pope-
emperor axis became like a see-saw: if one city was
Guelph the other was automatically Ghibelline. Conflict
between the cities began in 1141, ending only with a

SIENA

(*Opposite*) Siena:
the west front of the
Duomo and the
Campanile.

85

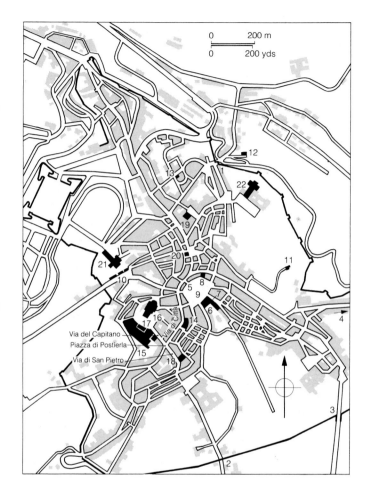

peace, to the northern city's advantage, in 1235. But it was a peace that benefited Sienese commercial and artisan interests, which managed to carve a place for themselves in the government of the city, hitherto in the hands of a landowning nobility. This new government took the city on to new heights of prosperity and renewed the struggle with Florence, which had its eye on Siena's coastal cities. The Florentines were beaten twice when they came against the Sienese, on the second occasion decisively at the battle of Montaperti, fought on 4 September 1260, when some 10,000 Florentine soldiers were killed and 15,000 taken prisoner.

The triumph was short-lived. The banking cities found that the success of Ghibellinism had its negative aspect, when in 1261 Pope Urban IV began to forbid their creditors to repay debts to the supporters of an excommunicate emperor. With the end of the Hohenstaufen line in 1268 the Sienese had lost their principal political support. On 11 June 1269 they were defeated in the field by the Florentines, the leader of their Ghibelline movement killed. From then until 1355 the city had a Guelph government, progressively reduced in the number of its members from 36 to nine. During this time relations with Florence improved and the city once again prospered. Most of the architecture we see today was built during these years. But towards the middle of the 14th century the same famine, over-taxation and disease that was affecting most other central Italian cities also hit Siena. The nobility took advantage of these misfortunes to align itself with the poorer members of the city and overthrow the commune in 1355. A number of different forms of government were experimented with in quick succession, until the last of them called in the Milanese Visconti to become *signori* in 1399. Perhaps unluckily from a strictly economic point of view this did not last, and the next 150 years were spent in forming and reforming governmental systems. In the 1550s the city was besieged and taken by the Spanish, and Siena finally passed to the control of the Medici Cosimo I in 1559.

*   *   *

Siena is built on three hills, like a great inverted 'Y'. The limits of the Roman town correspond with the earliest known walled limits to the city, and occupied the western hill. The Duomo occupies the north of this old town, and a castle of some kind must have stood in the southern part. The old crossroads appears to have been at what is now the Piazza di Postierla. During the tenth and 11th centuries a new town grew up to the east of these walls, and later a strip development had extended the city north in the Camollía district. By the early 13th century all these

87

areas had been enclosed by a new set of walls, and a second set went up later in the same century. Some of the old walling and a gate can be seen at the **Porta Ovile**. Other gates are the **Porta Tufi** of 1325 and the **Porta Romana** of 1327, both designed by Agnolo di Ventura, and the **Porta Pispini**, by Minuccio di Rinaldo in 1326.

THE CAMPO

Siena's great civic square, the Campo, is therefore not an accident of urban history, the growth of a public space on the site of a Roman forum. It represents the dragging of the city centre away from the ecclesiastical precinct and the assertion of the medieval city as independent entity. Until the mid-13th century the Campo was divided in two by a row of houses running north to south. At least part of it was a market that had grown up outside the eastern gate of the old walls. Some give credit to Giovanni Pisano, who was certainly in Siena and at work on the design of the Duomo, for understanding the urban possibilities here, and for conceiving the shell-shaped space that is unique among civic piazzas. Since 1347 the brick paving has been divided into nine sections by lines of stone, to represent the government of the Nine, unified in front of the Palazzo Pubblico. The real significance of this piazza is that its existence as a place of social unity is matched by its existence as an architectural space that has been able to support variety and change in its development over the years. In fact civic statutes were enacted at the beginning – 1262 – to determine what sort of buildings and roads could and could not be made around the Campo, supplemented by a further set in 1297 setting out window types and forbidding balconies. (This latter prohibition has at some time lapsed, and several buildings in the Campo now have balconies.)

If the *contrade* united in the Campo it was often to do battle with one another, and this common use of public space as a neutral battleground has its survival in the Sienese Palio. Preparations for this horse-race go on for months, jockeys and horses being bought and sold for enormous sums, until on the day of the race the horses are taken into local chapels and blessed, before being taken out to participate in a race of incredible violence. This is not sport: it is ritual warfare, where the ritual part is often lost sight of. The winning *contrada* decorates its streets and invites its every member to a sit-down celebration dinner, held at one long table in a city street. These matters should not be excluded from architectural discussion simply because they are ill-suited to art-historical analysis. Because they have to do with city spaces and with civilization, they are very much the subject matter of architecture.

The Palazzo Pubblico itself is a patchwork of additions and alterations, having grown with the city's government. In 1284 the commune's offices consisted of a single-storey stone building with a wooden roof, the central lower section of the present building, already with its 'Sienese arches', a segmental arch within a pointed arch. This building accommodated a mint and residential quarters for a few officials. Council meetings were at that time held in various palazzi throughout the town. It was decided in 1293 that this situation should not continue, and although some officials objected to the expense of building new premises, work was begun in 1285 to add a storey to the existing structure, and by the end of the century a third storey had been built; both these were of brick. In 1305 the top battlemented storey was put up, with nine merlons on front and sides to represent the government of the Nine who ruled the city at the time, and by 1310 two flanking wings of two storeys were added (each of three bays' width).

The next phase of work took the building farther east, with a new prison (1327), council hall (Salone del Gran Consiglio, 1330–42) and offices for the Podestà. The great tower of the **Mangia** (called after one of its bell-ringers, surnamed *Mangiaguadagni*: Spendthrift, or literally, Earnings-eater), founded in 1326, was completed in 1341. The work of the brothers Minuccio and Francesco di Rinaldo, that tower was simply the largest and most beautiful among the dozens of family towers of the Sienese houses, asserting the commune's existence as the

PALAZZO
PUBBLICO

89

'family of families', with greater rights and powers than any individual clan.

And that is where the medieval Palazzo Pubblico stopped, a great jagged pile on the skyline. Additions were made to the 'wings' in the 17th century that tended to even out the skyline and stress the horizontal elements of the group, and the eastern bell-tower was added to the central building in the following century to make it a symmetrical composition. They must have found the restless verticality – the Gothic – irritating.

The interiors of this building, or complex of buildings, are very largely intact, presenting a unique experience of medieval architecture in the number and variety of its rooms, not to mention the richness of their decoration. Every wall here is conceived as a surface for painting. In the great Sala del Mappamondo, so called from a now-lost rotating map of the world, painted by Lorenzetti, is Simone Martini's famous *Maestà* (1315), in fact not a fresco because painted onto dry plaster, and once liberally decorated with gold: an impressive piece of work, even if the peaceful sentiments it expressed on behalf of the commune were soon betrayed by another of the city's many civil wars.

An achievement more evidently civic is Simone's later *Guidoriccio da Fogliano* (1328), a fresco portrait of the *condottiere* leader of Sienese forces. As John White has so well pointed out, the painting is a vivid and extreme combination of realism and fantasy, with life-like horse and rider in an indeterminate relationship with the uninhabited cities and encampments that are their background.

Then, within the Sala della Pace, are Ambrogio Lorenzetti's great frescoes illustrating good and bad government. Apart from their astonishing compositional qualities, these paintings offer a wealth of information about the customs and practices of medieval times, from house-building to cultivation of fields. Bad Government has not lasted as well as Good Government, justice at least finding a place in art.

In the semicircle of buildings that encloses the Campo are a number of palazzi. Starting at the east, there is the

Palazzo Chigi-Zondadari, heavily rebuilt medieval, followed by **Palazzo Sansedoni**, an impressive work in brick and terracotta put up in the 1200s and enlarged in 1339. As a private house it once had a tower rivalling the Mangia in height. Other palazzi round the Campo are mostly later rebuildings of medieval work.

Also in the Campo is the famous **Fonte Gaia**, the Gay Fountain, so called because the population were so delighted by the arrival of water in the piazza in the 14th century. The remnants of Jacopo della Quercia's beautiful sculpture for this fountain, executed between 1409 and 1419, can be seen in the Palazzo Pubblico.

Water, always a problem for this hilltop city, meant that fountains took on a great importance, and were given emphasis in the fabric of the city by architectural means. Most impressive are the **Fonte Branda**, a massive structure with Gothic arches of 1246, the **Fonti di Follónica** of 1249, the **Fonte d'Ovile** of 1262 and the 14th-century **Fonte Nuova**. In the last years of the 13th century the commune instigated a search for the underground river, the Diana, that was commonly thought to flow beneath Siena. The result was the sinking of some 20 wells by 1309, doubling the city's total.

North of the Campo, Via di Città, lined with numerous palazzi from the 13th and 14th centuries (including the lovely **Palazzo Chigi-Saracini**, 12th to 14th centuries), makes an ogee curve westward towards the 'Roman' town. From the Piazza di Postierla, Via del Capitano leads north past the ex-**Palazzo del Capitano del Popolo** (late 13th century), now part of the university, and into the Piazza del Duomo, site of one of the most extraordinary building programmes in late medieval times. The present cathedral was begun, on the site of an older church, around 1150. In 1196 the works were given into the charge of a special committee of citizens, the Opera di Santa Maria, and later (1238–85) monks from the Cistercian house of San Galgano took over. The nave was completed around 1215, and the hexagonal **cupola** between 1259 and 1264. The building was then faced in banded marble along

THE DUOMO

Siena: Duomo
1. Cupola
2. Baptistry
3. 14th-century nave
4. Pulpit

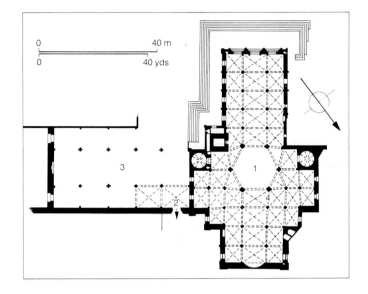

Siena: detail of the
sculpture, copies of
Giovanni Pisano's
work, on the
cathedral façade.

Pisan lines. It was for this church, with a barrel-vault roof and short chancel, that Giovanni Pisano built the lower part of the façade between 1284 and 1296.

Not long after, in 1317, the city decided to amplify the structure, extending the chancel east, building a new **baptistry** below it to act as a foundation. This technically difficult work went slowly, and when a commission of experts was called to report in 1322 they declared the foundations and the general scheme to be unsound. Indeed, declared the Sienese architect on the committee, if a grander building were required, it would be much better to pull down the whole building and start again. I suppose he may have been hoping for the job himself, but the city completed the work, and it has stood up well enough for six hundred years.

Perhaps they took confidence from this enterprise to make their next move. The new cathedral at Orvieto was more impressive than their own, which was anyway too small for their needs. The Florentines were building a monstrously large Duomo. Siena too would expand its religious centrepiece, and turn it into the largest church in all Italy. By 1339 the city had decided to turn the existing cathedral into the transepts of a much larger building, whose nave would run into it from the south. This unbelievably ambitious plan was actually begun, and part of the **nave** can be seen today as the Piazza Jacopo della Quercia. But the structural arrangements were so feeble that the building was obviously unstable. The disasters of mid-century brought the work to a halt, and the unsafe parts were demolished in 1357. How they had hoped to deal with the difficulties presented by the crossing and dome are unknown, but then this cavalier attitude, as we have seen in Florence, was common enough at the time.

Miriam by Giovanni Pisano, formerly on the cathedral façade (Museo dell'Opera Metropolitana, Siena).

In these same years the barrel vault was stripped off the nave, which was heightened. As a result, Giovanni Pisano's façade no longer fitted the building, and the upper part was rebuilt starting in 1376. The inspiration is Orvieto's highly decorated Gothic, but unfortunately Giovanni's façade was ill-suited to the attempt. Hence the complete lack of vertical continuity between upper and lower sections and a good deal of crowded detail around the edges. Giovanni's façade is in itself a sculptural masterpiece. The individual works of statuary have been replaced, and the originals can be seen in the Museo dell'Opera Metropolitana.

The interior of the cathedral has something of the oriental about it, with its emphatically striped columns, and an airiness, resulting from the peculiarities of its dome construction, that interrupts the expected rectilinearity of the building. This is a hexagonal structure, wider than the nave but not quite wide enough to cover the transepts as well. Nor is it central to the crossing, and its eccentricity begins to give a rotational movement to the architectural space. The eye is constantly drawn through arches and past columns, into voids, and more arches.

Siena: the interior of the Duomo, looking east down the nave.

Among the many wonders of painting and sculpture in this building, the **pulpit** of Nicola Pisano must be picked out for special mention. Nicola was Giovanni's father. In 1260 he had carved the pulpit for the Duomo at Pisa, and now here he was in 1266 carrying out a similar commission at Siena. The former work is an excellent interpretation of antique classical sculpture as found on Roman sarcophagi, adapted as best possible to Christian purposes. Now, in six

Siena: the Palazzo Buonsignori, housing the Pinacoteca Nazionale.

years, Nicola had developed sculpture into a medium independent of the old forms, with a naturalism and grace that, when the two are compared, seem almost wholly absent in the Pisa work.

West of the Duomo is the **Spedale di Santa Maria della Scala** (referring to the *scala* or stairs in front of the Duomo). The foundation is of uncertain date but the exterior of the present building dates from the 12th and 13th centuries.

From the Piazza del Duomo, across the Piazza di Postierla, Via di San Pietro runs south to the Palazzo Buonsignori, a battlemented house, in fact built in the early 1400s, yet firmly in the late Gothic tradition. One of Siena's finest palazzi, the building now houses the **Pinacoteca Nazionale**, a superb collection of paintings from the 12th to the 17th centuries, among which are examples of the work of Duccio, Bartolo di Fredi, the brothers Lorenzetti and Simone Martini.

OTHER BUILDINGS OF IMPORTANCE IN SIENA

Palazzo Salimbeni, Piazza Salimbene: 14th-century house, now belonging to the Monte dei Paschi, the oldest Italian bank. (It seems that when they began they guaranteed their operations using the pasture [*paschi*] rents of land owned in the Maremma.) The interior can be visited, and the storage areas of the old house have recently been restored.

Palazzo Tolomei, Banchi di Sopra. A stone building in Siena is unusual. This is the oldest surviving house in the city, built in 1205, but rebuilt – except for the ground floor – in 1267.

San Domenico, Piazza San Domenico. Located on a promontory west of the medieval wall, the severe and powerful church of San Domenico was begun in the early 14th century and completed in 1465. This is of course a mendicant church, with an Egyptian cross plan and square apse. Its immense height and rigorous logic betray Cistercian influence, and almost as if religious principles were being directly converted into architectural principles, the building is an embodiment of simplicity, strength and grandeur. Unusually, transepts are higher than nave, and this is expressed externally by a continuous pitched roof running from one end to the other. Internally these transepts form one space, and it is the nave itself that is separated from them by an arch. The church is brick, with timber roofs, and internal black and white banding.

San Francesco, Piazza San Francesco. This church, founded in 1326 and also of brick, is closer in feeling to Santa Croce in Florence, with continuous nave and transepts divided off by arches. Compared to San Domenico it is much lower, a more 'Italian' type of Gothic. Site levels, always a problem on Siena's hilly terrain, are used here to create gentle plane differences between nave and transepts, transepts and chapels. Here too the interior space is given the black and white zebra treatment.

Asciano, N.348, east of Siena. The town became a Sienese possession in 1285, and was subsequently fortified. The walls have gone but there are many medieval buildings, including the **Collegiata di Sant'Agata**, 11th-century Romanesque, and a good collection of Sienese paintings in the Museo di Arte Sacra.

OTHER TOWNS AND ISOLATED BUILDINGS

Abbazia di Monte Oliveto Maggiore, N.451. In 1313 Bernardo Tolomei, professor of law and member of a powerful Sienese family, abandoned the world and came to this isolated place, known as the Desert of Accona. The land belonged to his family. From 1319, when the Church gave its approval for the order of Olivetans, a variant of the Benedictine rule, this monastery and the order generally grew quickly. Most of the buildings are 15th-century and later, but even so many of these carry on a style of earlier times.

Cuna, off the N.2. This building was the grange or farm belonging to the Spedale di Santa Maria della Scala in Siena, which took possession of it in the 13th century.

The apse of the Abbazia di Sant'Ántimo.

Abbazia di Sant'Ántimo: detail of a column capital.

Entirely built of brick, it is a rare example of a fortified medieval farm. It is in effect a small town, with walls and towers, and medieval buildings in a perfect state of preservation.

Buonconvento, N.2. The town has a rectilinear plan, with walls of 1300. It was an important defensive point for the Sienese.

Montalcino, west of the N.2. The town, once a free commune, was taken by Siena after the battle of Montaperti (1260). In 1361 the Sienese built the Rocca, making it one of the chief defensive points of their republic. The Piazza del Popolo, Palazzo Comunale (13th to 14th centuries) and the Rocca are all worth seeing.

Abbazia di Sant'Ántimo, west of the N.2, south of Montalcino. Founded, according to legend, by Charlemagne, this Benedictine abbey became in late medieval times an immensely powerful feudal landlord, perhaps the largest in the neighbourhood of Siena, with which it came into conflict in the early years of the 13th century. By the end of the century its power had been reduced and it was suppressed altogether in 1462. The church itself is Cistercian Romanesque of the late 12th century, with a semicircular apse and no transepts. Outside and inside are faced in travertine, with decorative work in onyx, quarried nearby at Castelnuovo. The combination produces a subtle luminescence.

San Quírico d'Orcia, N.2. The Romanesque **Collegiata**, or Pieve di Osenna, was founded in the eighth century and largely rebuilt in the 12th and 13th. The town also has several medieval secular buildings near the Palazzo Pretorio, as well as the church of Santa Maria (11th to 12th centuries).

Rocca d'Orcia, west of the N.2. Ruins of a 14th-century castle, highly picturesque, in this medieval town.

Abbadia San Salvatore, off the N.2. The abbey was

founded in the eighth century, and grew rapidly, becoming at one time the richest in all Tuscany. It was first Benedictine, then Camaldulian and finally Cistercian from 1228 until suppressed in 1782. The church was built in 1036, with the addition of a sacristy in the late 1200s. The plan is a Latin cross, the nave tall.

Through the Porta della Badia is the **Borgo Medioevale**, a large and fascinating example, nearly complete, of a fortified medieval mountain town.

Pitigliano, N.74. The town seems to grow out of the ground as an extension of the rock itself. The city is virtually a Renaissance rebuilding of a medieval plan.

Sovana, off the N.74, north of Pitigliano. A powerful town in medieval times, reduced by war and malaria, Sovana even today is partly abandoned. Its bishopric was moved to Pitigliano in 1660. There is a wonderful old Palazzo Pretorio of the 13th century.

Sorano, off the N.74, north of Pitigliano. A walled medieval town built on a rocky outcrop.

Sovana: a door in the flank wall of the Duomo.

THE EAST
AREZZO AND SOUTH-EAST OF FLORENCE

Arezzo sits on a hill overlooking the plain where three rivers meet: the Valdarno, the Cassentino and the Valdichiana, and it owes its existence largely to its position on the communication route between Rome, Florence and the Romagna, both a trade and a defensive position. Of the Roman city little remains after the barbarian invasions. Vie Pelliceria and Fontanella, and the Via Pescioni that crosses it, mark Roman roads, but there is not much else. It would seem that the inhabitants abandoned the Roman town and moved within the earlier Etruscan walls for safety.

Later the city's bishops became immensely important, in fact occupying the role of feudal lords of Arezzo and its *contado* from 1052 on. The town grew in the 11th century, when new walls were built in the north-east corner of the city, taking in roughly the area where the Duomo and Fortezza stand. But in the days when the city was a free commune, from 1098 when the first Consoli were elected, it took a great leap forward in population and wealth, so that a new set of walls was needed around 1200. The south-western limit of these walls can be traced in the present Via Garibaldi, that sweeps around the south and west sides of the city. On the north they joined up with the older walls. The enclosed area had trebled from 17 to 51 hectares (42 to 126 acres). The main axis of the city now shifted from Via Ricasoli to the Borgo Maestro (the present Corso Italia). Throughout the 13th century the city filled with tower-houses and new churches, and the wars with Florence and Siena continued. It will illustrate the difficulty of neatly summarizing the politics of these city-states to say that Arezzo was a Ghibelline city led by bishops, and was attacked by the combined armies of Siena (Ghibelline) and Florence (Guelph). The Aretini held the combination at bay in 1287–8, only to be crushed

(*Opposite*) Poppi: general view.

99

the following year by the Florentines, who killed the city's bishop and military leader, Guiglielmino Ubertini.

Most famous of these warrior prelates was Guido Tarlati, elected bishop in 1312 and *signore* – in effect, an elected feudal lord – for life in 1321. He led Arezzo's forces in conquest of many of the surrounding towns and castles, and the city to even greater heights of wealth and power. Under his rulership the city walls were rebuilt on the south-east – roughly where the existing though later walls still stand – doubling the city's enclosed area. After Tarlati's death in 1328 the city found itself unable to hold on to the gains it had made. It was actually sold to Florence in 1337, and having lost its political independence became a prey to other and stronger cities. Having been passed about, it was sold for a second time to the Florentines in 1384, and on this occasion it was stripped of every element of self-government. The existing walls were built in the 16th century, but over the following centuries the population fell, increasing again only with the arrival of the railway in the 19th century. The city's major

Arezzo: Piazza Grande, with the apse of Santa Maria della Pieve on the right.

growth, however, has been industrial, since the Second World War.

The two most important medieval monuments in Arezzo are found together: **Piazza Grande** and the Pieve. The piazza was first planned out around the year 1200, and is remarkable for the way in which its awkward slope has been managed, as well as for the buildings around it. Many of these houses, on the east and south, are quite ordinary for the most part but retain the wooden balconies with their 45° timber strut supports that could come straight from the axonometric constructions of late medieval frescoes: the work of Giotto and Ambrogio Lorenzetti. On the west are the apse of Santa Maria della Pieve (13th-century), the 18th-century Palazzo dei Tribunale, and the Palazzo della Fraternità dei Laici, begun in 1375. Giorgio Vasari, who was from Arezzo and kept a house here, designed the long, arcaded Palazzo delle Logge (1573) that closes the northern side of the piazza.

Around the corner in Corso Italia is the entrance to the **Pieve**, one of the finest Romanesque buildings in Tuscany, all the more interesting for being relatively complete. The present building was begun in 1140 as the refacing of an older church, but clearly one thing led to another, and when the scaffolding came down in the early 1300s, the older building had disappeared. In its arcading the façade (early 1200s) shows the influence of the Pisa-Lucca prototypes, yet it is not a copy. Five blind arches at ground level are topped with three straight levels of arcading, without the usual sloping extremities where the aisle roofs pitch towards the nave, and this gives a thoroughly classical feeling to the composition. Among the wide variety on display, standing like a sample shop of column types, the 16th column from the left along the top row is indeed a caryatid. The main entrance portal is decorated with lovely reliefs depicting the months of the year, carved by an unknown hand in the 13th century. Each of the lunettes over the three doors also has relief carving, dating from around 1227.

The church's belfry, with the disposition of its 40 openings lightening the apparent mass of the structure, is set back from the façade, though a giant pilaster has been

Arezzo: the façade of Santa Maria della Pieve.

added to fill the re-entrant angle at ground level, and carried up the full height of the belfry. It was completed in 1330.

The interior shows a move towards the Gothic in the pointing of nave arches, although the older part at the east end shows round-headed arches. A dome was intended but only the blind arcading was completed. The complex of elements that make up the east end of the church produces one of the most satisfying works of architecture in central Italy.

Corso Italia continues north to become Via dei Pileati. Here are the Palazzo Pretorio, mostly 15th-century and later, and remains of the Palazzo del Capitano del Popolo (1278) and other medieval buildings. To the west, on a great stepped podium of the 16th century and rather isolated from the rest of the city, stands the **Duomo**, a bit of a mixed bag. The building was begun about 1280 and was not finished until some two and a half centuries later. But then the façade is 20th-century gothic, put up in 1901–14, and the belfry was built in 1857–9. It is for the works of art it contains as much as for its own fabric that the Duomo is worth a visit. In the southern aisle, second bay from the east end, is the **Cappella di Ciuccio Tarlati**, 1334, with frescoes. In the eastern chapel is the **Arca di San Donato**, a beautifully carved 14th-century marble box, standing on 12 columns and pilasters, in which the ashes of the city's patron saint are kept. This is the work of Agostino di Giovanni and Agnolo di Ventura. On the north, also by these artists, though perhaps working to the designs of Giotto, is the great **monument** to Guido Tarlati, carved with 16 bas-reliefs of the bishop's life.

Via Ricasoli leads west, and Via di Sasso Verde runs north of it to the Piazza Fossombroni. Both have fragments of medieval houses, and the piazza has the church of **San Domenico**, founded in 1275 by the Tarlati family, designed, according to Vasari, by Nicola Pisano, and completed within 25 years. The plain façade is a peculiar asymmetrical affair, the belfry rising high on the right while the cornice of the left side falls away with the aisle roof. The interior is a plain but luminous space, covered in fresco work, but the masterpiece of the building is Cimabue's *Crucifix*, a youthful work painted around 1260.

Back along Via Ricasoli, Via Cisalpino leads south to Piazza San Francesco, the present-day centre of Arezzo. The church of **San Francesco** stood outside the first medieval walls (Via Cavour) and was only enclosed by the second ring of 1200 (Via Garibaldi). As usual it was the mendicant church and its associated convent that crystallized new developments outside the gates of the older town. Unfortunately the piazza was enlarged in the 19th century at the expense of the convent, which lost a wing to Via Guido Monaco, so that all medieval spatial relationships have disappeared.

There would be something slightly fatuous about describing this church and failing to mention its greatest glory, the fresco cycle by Piero della Francesca, though it falls outside our period. The frescoes do, however, illustrate the medieval Legend of the Cross, passed on by Jacopo da Voragine, or Varagine, in his book *The Golden Legend*. The paintings were made in the years 1453–64. The church itself is of the usual Franciscan simplicity: plain façade (rebuilt in the 14th century) and inside a single nave with pointed arches.

Arezzo: the façade of San Francesco.

CORTONA

Medieval Cortona grew up in the western part of the large area enclosed by the Etruscans in the fourth century BC. Much of this medieval city still exists, the sandstone houses, with their wooden balconies, filling in a street pattern whose irregularity derives from the steeply sloping site.

The city had its commune from the 12th to the 14th century, but was not large enough to resist the Aretini, who sacked it in 1258. Still, the town made its alliances and did well enough for itself, becoming a bishopric in 1325. In the same year the family Ranieri dei Casali was appointed *signore*, and the family kept the title until 1409. Two years after this it was in Florentine hands.

All the medieval public buildings have been so much altered as to be hardly medieval at all – and although that cannot be used as a criticism of them as buildings (in a way the reverse is true, as it proves them to have been useful over many centuries), it means there is little point in describing them in any detail. Cortona is a city for an afternoon's stroll.

At the centre of the city is the Piazza della Repubblica, with the Palazzo del Capitano del Popolo (13th-century, transformed in the 15th) and opposite the Palazzo Comunale (1241 and much altered) with its set of broad steps. To the right of these, Piazza Signorelli opens to the north, with the **Palazzo Pretorio** at No.9, built by the Casali family in the 1200s. Only the flank wall of this structure remains, in Via Casali, decorated with the arms of the various *capitani* and *commissari* who lived in the buildings subsequently. From the Piazza Signorelli, past the theatre, one of the city's finest streets, the **Via Dardano**, continues north. Several of the houses are medieval. Beyond the Porta Colonia are stretches of medieval wall, built on top of the massive blocks that make up the Etruscan walls.

Several other streets have interesting medieval houses: Via Berrettini, running north past the Palazzo del Pretorio; Via Roma, west from Piazza della Repubblica; and Via Janelli, in the quarter south of Via Roma.

OTHER TOWNS AND ISOLATED BUILDINGS

The area east and south of Florence is dotted with isolated buildings of considerable interest, not least a great number of monastic buildings.

Lucignano, between the N.73, N.326 and the Autostrada del Sole. The town, with a commanding view of the Valdichiana, is built on an unusual elliptical medieval plan, essentially a piazza and public buildings in the centre and rings of streets about. The medieval walls are almost wholly intact, and the tall **Cassero tower** (14th-century) can be climbed for a wonderful view of the surrounding landscape. In the centre of town, the 14th-century **Palazzo Comunale** has recently been restored. To its left, at a lower level, is the 13th-century church of **San Francesco**, grey and white stripes with a Gothic door and rose window. The inside is decorated with Sienese frescoes.

Castello di Trebbio, north of the N.69. A very good example of 13th-century fortification, largely intact.

San Giovanni Valdarno, N.69. Arnolfo di Cambio is said to have given this town its rectilinear plan in the 14th century. The **Palazzo Pretorio**, also said to be his design, has been very much altered. There are one or two medieval buildings, including the little 13th-century church of **Santa Lucia** in Via Alberti, with frescoes of the following century.

Terranuova Bracciolini, east of the N.69. Another rectilinear plan attributed to Arnolfo. Parts remain of the walls built by Florence in 1337, though the gates were all destroyed in World War II.

Cennina, off the N.540. This small town huddles around the ruined keep of a 12th-century castle that once belonged to the Tarlati. Its modest central piazza is 15th-century but in the medieval tradition.

Castiglion Fiorentino, N.71. The city is still walled (13th- and 14th-century), and has the remains of an 11th- and 12th-century keep. In Via Dante is the church of Sant' Agostino, early 1300s. At No.16, Vicolo Cassuci, is the former church of San Lazzo in Santa Stefano of 1350, entirely covered inside with frescoes of the same date. At the end of Corso Italia is the 14th-century Porta Fiorentina, and near to that the church of San Francesco, Romanesque with Gothic overtones, late 1200s. Inside are some fine frescoes of *c.* 1290.

Castello di Montecchio Vesponi, N.71. A stone's throw from Castiglion Fiorentino, this castle has complete battlemented walls and towers. The Florentines gave it to the English mercenary adventurer John Hawkwood (who became Giovanni Acuto) in the 14th century. As it stands the castle is of 13th-century construction.

Vallombrosa, off the N.70. The medieval architecture here is limited to the monastery belfry (13th-century) and the Paradisino, of 1227 and after. But the importance of the place should be seen in other terms. It was here that Giovanni Gualberto, offspring of a noble Florentine family, came about 1028 and lived with several others in huts of branches for seven years. Eventually he obtained papal sanction for his order of monks, the Vallombrosians. This order, a more austere interpretation of the Benedictine rule, was eventually to predominate in Tuscany. The monastic buildings standing today are extensive amplifications of a simple idea that was cultivated, precisely, far from cities and architecture. The architecture of Gualberto was branches and leaves, and in the Vallombrosa you can be closer to a medieval environment than you can be in Florence, or as a matter of fact, any other city.

Some have seen the formation of monastic movements as a repossession by the landed nobility of the countryside, an assertion of their rights there and a rejection of the city.

Grópina: the apse of San Pietro.

Grópina, east from Montevarchi on the N.69: a remarkable parish church, **San Pietro**, built around 1000. The inside is a basilica plan, nave and two aisles with a round arcaded apse. The column capitals are carved with strange historical reliefs.

Grópina: the *ambo*, or pulpit of San Pietro.

La Verna, N.208. This striking part of Tuscany is famous for its natural beauty but more so because of its associations with St Francis, who received the stigmata here in 1224. Buildings to see include the church of Santa Maria degli Angeli, 1216–18, and later enlarged; the Chiesa Maggiore, or Basilica, begun 1348; the Church of the Stigmata, 1263; and the cell of St Francis.

Poppi, N.70. This pretty town has a splendid Palazzo Pretorio, begun towards the end of the 12th century as a castle, rebuilt in 1274 and later enlarged, possibly by Arnolfo di Cambio. The older part is to the right of the tall tower. There is also the fine church of San Fedele, 1185–95. There are many interesting towns near Poppi, in the beautiful area known as the Casentino. At **Castel San**

Niccolò is the Romanesque San Martino a Vado of the 11th and 12th centuries, and the pretty Piazza della Fiera. **San Pietro di Romena** has one of the most interesting parish churches in the area, dating from the 12th century. **Castello di Romena** presents the ruins of a once magnificent castle first erected around the year 1000. Three of its 14 towers remain, and the view from this site is exceptional.

Monastero/Eremo di Camaldoli, north of the N.71. San Romualdo founded the monastic order of the Camaldolesi (Camaldulians) here in 1027. The monastery today is largely post-14th-century, but the Eremo is a rare example of a medieval type of monastic layout. Beyond the Chiesa di Salvatore, behind an iron gate, and forbidden to women, are 20 cells arranged in five rows. Only the so-called Pope's Chapel is medieval (1227), the others being heavy restorations or reconstructions.

Caprese Michelangelo, off the N.208: a 14th-century Palazzo del Podestà, where Michelangelo was born on 6 March 1475.

Gargonza, N.73. A tiny medieval town complete with its battlemented walls and entrance gate. It has a lovely piazza, with a tower on one side and a Romanesque church on the other. Nearby are the ruins of a second Romanesque church.

Civitella in Val di Chiana, north of the N.73: a walled medieval city. The Porta Senese is almost complete, the 13th-century castle is not, but makes a picturesque ruin. Many people were killed and buildings destroyed on 29 June 1944.

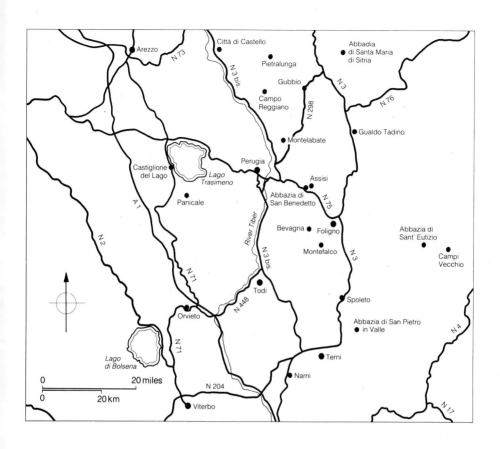

UMBRIA

In most respects Umbria presents a completely different picture from Tuscany. The name derives from the Umbri, a people coeval with the Etruscans; but their territory does not correspond with the present region, nor does the sixth Augustan region of *Umbria*, which on the west was limited by the Tiber (so excluding Perugia) and on the east ran to the Adriatic. Diocletian divided the area between Tuscia and Flaminia, and the name disappeared from use until the 17th century. In the 19th it was revived as an administrative region, its boundaries finally settled in 1927.

The critical fact about Umbria in early medieval history is that it lies between Rome and the Exarchate of Ravenna, which owed allegiance to the Roman emperor in Constantinople. It was formed to defend the Empire against the Lombards, who invaded Italy from the fifth century, settling and forming feudal states. In time only a thin strip of land remained to connect Ravenna proper with Rome: the area west of the Tiber, Perugia and its territories. Hence the west of Umbria, caught between the Lombard Duchies of Tuscany and Spoleto, developed to some degree in isolation. All this matters somewhat less in late medieval times, when the great feudal domains were being broken up by the city-states, when monastic orders imposed uniformity over much of the administrative, agricultural and artistic life of the country, and when artists began travelling to distant cities and regions to practise their crafts.

Yet from a geographical point of view Umbria remains divided, split from north to south by the upper Tiber. To its west, tributary rivers are short and torrential, the hard surface geology of sandstone and marl not favouring agriculture, though providing excellent building stone. East of the Tiber, limestone is the geological base, with long and comparatively slow-flowing rivers giving good drainage and good natural irrigation.

(*Opposite*) Map of Umbria.

109

THE NORTH
PERUGIA AND GUBBIO

Since Etruscan times Perugia has been an important commercial centre, controlling the communications routes of the upper Tiber valley. These same routes led the barbarian tribes to its gates in the sixth century. Following a long siege, the city was taken and destroyed by Totila in 547, and for the next five hundred years Perugia's history is unknown. But in the 11th century things changed, as the commune was formed, and the city, by successfully warring against its neighbours, came to dominate a large part of Umbria. Perugia was mostly Guelph, accepting the papacy's protection while rejecting its *signoria*, or feudal domination. Its vicinity to Rome and position on the road to Ravenna made the city a favourite with the popes, several of whom had palazzi here. Life was on the whole safer in Perugia than in a Rome constantly shaken by political agitation.

Towards the end of the 14th century this papal alliance changed. Martin IV excommunicated the whole population for having ruthlessly devastated the nearby city of Foligno. In 1369 the pope won a military victory over the Perugini and made them accept his *signoria*. Revolution was, as it so often is, followed by civil war, and the city rapidly headed towards permanent domination by outsiders. Perugia was passed between various families in the 15th century before being forcibly taken once more by the papacy in 1530, remaining part of the papal dominion until the 19th century.

*   *   *

The physical city of Perugia consists of the central hilltop on which the Etruscan town was built, a tri-lobed plan, and three 'arms' that radiate from it: to the north-east, Corso Bersaglieri; to the north-west, Corso Garibaldi; and to the south-east, Corso Cavour. The Etruscan walls

(Opposite) Perugia: the Via Ritorta.

Perugia
1. Fontana Maggiore
2. Cattedrale
3. Palazzo Comunale (dei Priori)
4. Via Volte della Pace
5. Porta della Mandorla
6. Torre dei Donati
7. Torre degli Sciri
8. Via Bagliona
9. Case di Gentile Baglioni
10. Sant'Ercolano
11. San Domenico
12. San Pietro
13. Santa Giuliana

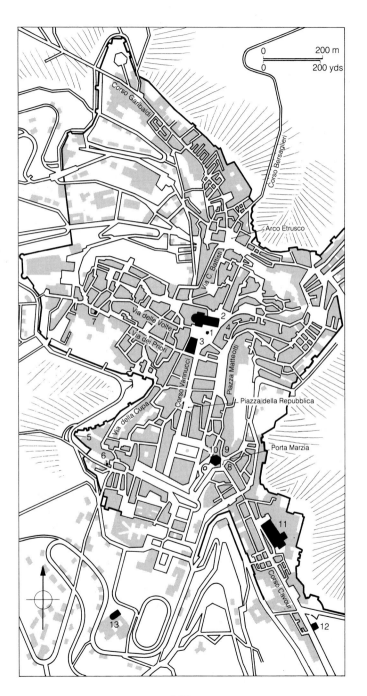

can be traced as follows: from Porta Marzia, to Porta di Sant'Ercolano, Porta Sole, the Arco Etrusco, then following Via C. Battisti, west, then south to the Torre degli Sciri and east again, following Via di Cupa to the Porta della Mandorla and the Torre dei Donati. These walls, made from enormous irregular blocks into what is known as cyclopean masonry, enclosed space enough for Perugia until the final years of the 13th century. New walls were begun in 1321, extending the city along the three arms already mentioned. The greatest change to the urban fabric from that time until this century was the construction, beginning in 1540, of the Rocca Paolina, the fortress with which the papacy was to control Perugia, and for which many towers and houses belonging to families that had fought the papacy were knocked down. What remains is a city whose streets run on steep slopes, with ramps in brick and stone, with medieval and Etruscan gates, arched streets, and the sudden contrast between cramped lanes and vast panoramas over the surrounding countryside.

At the very heart of Perugia, in the Piazza Novembre IV, stands the famous **Fontana Maggiore** (circa 1277), perhaps the most lovely of all medieval fountains. It is the work of Fra' Bevignate of Perugia and Boninsegna from Venice, who collaborated on the technical and hydraulic aspects of the work, and of Nicola and Giovanni Pisano, who designed the architectural scheme and made the sculptural reliefs. Although this fountain lies close to the ground, without exuberant verticals, it is not a static composition. At the top of a stepped plinth sits the lower basin, a 25-sided polygon. Each facet is separated from its neighbour by a group of three columns, and divided into two relief panels. Within that basin stands a second, supported by columns. This is made up of 12 concave panels, in which full sculptural figures appear, as if the background of a relief panel had bowed back, allowing the figures to stand fully in three dimensions. The 12–25 rhythm of the two basins, never allowing a congruence between panels, imparts a visual spin to the work, leading the eye up and down and always around the fountain. The subtleties of pink and white colouring are a beautiful compliment to this delicacy of movement.

Directly to the north of the Fontana Maggiore, on a high flight of steps, is the **Cattedrale** of San Lorenzo, planned in 1300 but only begun in 1345, to replace an earlier Romanesque building. Completed in 1490 and much altered since, the cathedral has little of medieval interest. Its partially completed façade was built in 1729.

But the **Palazzo Comunale**, or **dei Priori**, on the southern side of the piazza, among the finest of all Italian *palazzi pubblici*, more than makes up for a disappointing cathedral. The original building consisted of the first ten bays of the long façade and the first three bays of the short, and would not have had the cascading fan-shaped steps that descend to the piazza from the monumental entrance door. It was designed by two local men, Giacomo di Servadio and Giovanello di Benvenuto, work beginning in 1293 and finishing four years later. Not until 1328 were the neighbouring buildings bought up and demolished to make way for extensions, and these were carried out in the style of the original building, with the additions of the steps and balcony facing the piazza. The two most notable aesthetic features of the building

Perugia: the Palazzo Comunale.

114

(imagining the original structure) are its horizontal emphasis and its repetitive, evenly spaced window openings. The building is tall, but there are no continuous verticals in the composition, and any association of vertically aligned windows is denied by the broad expanses of bare stonework that separate them. Projecting cornices reinforce this. And whereas earlier palazzi had often depended on a solid block-like building to support an irregular disposition of openings, this façade is much reduced in visual weight by the long rhythmic stretch of tracery windows. In all this there is a hint of the Doge's palace in Venice (begun later, in 1309), married to the robust materials of central Italy: travertine, limestone and marble.

Above the door facing the piazza are two brackets, carrying chains and a pole from which were hung various signs of victory in war, most notably the keys of Siena after the battle of Torrita in 1358. The figures on the brackets are the griffin of Perugia and the Guelph lion, cast in bronze in the latter part of the 13th century and the earliest examples of large-scale bronze casting in Europe since ancient times. The door leads to the Sala dei Notari, but is no longer used.

The western face of the palazzo can be seen from the Via della Gabbia, so called because prisoners would be exposed here to public ridicule, hung in iron cages suspended from the building. The remains of various towers and other medieval buildings can be seen incorporated into this façade. Via dei Priori passes underneath the palazzo bell-tower and into Corso Vannucci. The door here leading into the Palazzo Comunale is really like something you would expect to find on a church, and gives a good idea of the displacement of values from the ecclesiastical to the urban institution at the time of its construction in the 1340s.

Inside this door is an austere atrium, and on the first floor the astonishing **Sala dei Notari**, formerly del Popolo. This room occupies the whole first floor of the original building (except for a staircase), and is divided into bays by huge semicircular arches that span the whole width of the room. Two levels of benches are built in on the long

Perugia: the Sala dei Notari in the Palazzo Comunale.

walls. The whole space is decorated with frescoes, begun in 1297 and carried on into the 16th century.

On the third floor of the palazzo is the Galleria Nazionale dell'Umbria, a collection of paintings and sculpture, much of it medieval, that should not be missed.

To the right of the great entrance door to the palazzo in Corso Vannucci, a smaller door leads to the **Sala del Collegio della Mercanzia**, given to the Arte dei Mercanti in 1390 for a meeting room and decorated by them in a late Gothic style in the 1400s.

To the east of Piazza Novembre IV runs the **Via Volte della Pace**, a long Gothic portico of the 14th century built on the remains of the Etruscan walls. Tradition has it that peace treaties between Perugia and her neighbouring cities were signed here, hence its name. The arches were originally open, but successive generations of builders have succeeded in closing them off.

116

South on Corso Vannucci is the Piazza della Repubblica, and to its west one of the oldest quarters of the city: in Via Luigi Bonazzi several 13th- and 14th-century houses and a Gothic arch over the street; at No.4 Via Cesare Caporali a 13th-century stone-built tower-house; Via della Cupa, which follows the Etruscan walls, and Via Annibale Mariotti; then Via Bruschi, full of medieval houses, which descends to the **Porta della Mandorla**, originally an Etruscan gate, reused and largely rebuilt in medieval times. From here the road leads down to the right, to the 14th-century **Torre dei Donati**.

Via dei Priori leads west from Piazza Novembre IV, with medieval houses and the **Torre degli Sciri**, 46m (151ft) high, probably 12th-century. Perugia, like most central Italian cities in medieval times, at one time had dozens of these tower-houses. Near the Duomo, to the north of Via dei Priori, is Via delle Volte. This 'street of arches' was once covered by a large Gothic hall, the remains of which still stand, conveying vividly an impression that one has about so much of Perugia, with its arches everywhere tying buildings together across streets, that it is one large edifice, a continuous building, some parts roofed as houses and some left open as streets.

At the bottom end of Corso Vannucci and to the east of Piazza Italia is the Porta Marzia and the entrance to the underground street of **Via Bagliona**, a peculiarly medieval environment. This is where the Rocca Paolina stood, and many of the buildings here are remains of the medieval houses demolished to make way for that papal castle. Beyond the Porta Marzia is the tower of the **Case di Gentile Baglioni** and the remains of various other medieval houses.

Perugia: the church of Sant'Ercolano.

Of churches there are few good examples to see. **Sant' Ercolano**, built on the old walls (1297–1326) by the Porta Marzia, is a striking polygonal structure with a gigantic pointed arch on each facet. Beneath the later plaster and frescoes on the inside the architectural form can still be perceived. The nave of **San Domenico**, begun in 1305, collapsed and was rebuilt in 1614, though one flank wall and the apse are of the original building. **San Pietro** has preserved much of its late tenth-century structure, but has an interior decorated in the 15th and 16th centuries. Only **Santa Giuliana**, Romanesque-Gothic of the mid-13th century said to have been designed by Gattapone, remains in a major degree a medieval building. Its façade is 14th-century, pink and white marble in delicate geometrical designs. Inside are frescoes of the 1200s and 1300s. A pretty cloister of 1375 is connected to the church.

GUBBIO

Gubbio stands on the edge of an upland plain at the foot of Monte Ingino, an Umbrian foundation, after that a Roman city, but in its aspect today a thoroughly medieval city. Its history in the Middle Ages is that of many another central Italian city: a commune established in the 11th century, improbable victories over enemies (Gubbio defeated an alliance of no less than 11 cities ranged against her in battle in 1151), and an age of growing wealth. From the middle of the 14th century things went downhill, with a succession of *signori* taking over, and the town finally asking the Montefeltro of Urbino to take over.

* * *

Gubbio has a simple but dramatic organizational scheme: five streets run roughly parallel, following the contours of the mountain at different levels. These are the Via XX Settembre, Via Savelli, Corso Garibaldi, Via Mazzini and Via Reposati, whose buildings, stacking up against the mountainside, produce a powerful architectural composition. Materials for construction are brick, and more frequently limestone, quarried locally.

(*Opposite*) Gubbio
1. San Francesco
2. San Giovanni
   Battista
3. Piazza della
   Signoria
4. Palazzo dei
   Consoli
5. Palazzo Pretorio
6. Via dei Consoli
7. Palazzo del
   Bargello
8. Duomo
9. Palazzo del
   Capitano del
   Popolo
10. Sant'Agostino

The best way to visit the city is to start at the bottom – the west side – and work uphill. Through the Porta degli Ortacci, Via Matteotti leads to a large piazza, with the church of **San Francesco** on the south. This is a basilica church, the typically plain mendicant layout, nave and two aisles, all very simply handled, and here with three polygonal apses at the eastern end. The polygonal belfry is of the same date as the church, 1259–92, but the interior has been altered, in particular by a substitution of the original open-truss wooden roof by a vaulted construction in the 17th century. Only the easternmost bay of the

original roof survives to convey some idea of the quality of the space. The northern apse is decorated with late Gothic frescoes (1408–13) by Gubbio's most famous painter, Ottaviano Nelli.

From the piazza, Via della Repubblica leads east and meets Via Camignano. Off this street is the 13th-century church of **San Giovanni Battista**, with a good and largely complete façade and belfry.

Via della Repubblica runs farther east to Via Baldassini. North along this street is the precipitous western face of the Palazzo Comunale, four stupendous arches that form part of a substructure supporting the Piazza della Signoria and Palazzo dei Consoli. On the left of the street is an almost continuous row of 13th- and 14th-century houses. At the top of the street, Via Gattapone doubles back and leads to the **Piazza della Signoria** itself.

What we are presented with here is a masterwork of architecture, a man-made landscape in which the piazza echoes the upland plane in front of it and the tall palazzi the mountains behind. If the Campo at Siena was made on the idea of enclosure, cutting off from view the valley opening south, Gubbio's architect aimed at an opposite result, elevating the complex and sitting it on top of the city.

The project seems to have been conceived by one man, Angelo da Orvieto, and built according to his plans between 1322 and 1349, though never finished. The largest building is the **Palazzo dei Consoli** (1322–37), possibly designed with the collaboration of Gattapone. As at the Perugian Palazzo Comunale, the first floor is wholly taken up by the vast barrel-vaulted **Salone**, a public meeting hall in medieval times. Leading to the Salone is a staircase consisting of a fan-shaped plinth from which a single flight of steps arches up, intersecting an arched balcony. The economy of this structure, in its ability to lighten the cliff-like façade behind it and give a sense of grace to the severity of the whole building, is an achievement of the highest order. The upper floors of the

Gubbio: Palazzo dei Consoli (left) and Palazzo Pretorio (right).

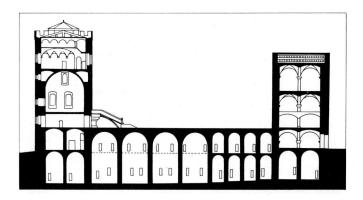

building house the Museo Civico and the Pinacoteca Comunale, both of which are full of interest. From the open loggia at the top there are exhilarating panoramic views of city and countryside.

At the other end of the piazza is the **Palazzo Pretorio**, finished in 1349, and possibly designed by Gattapone. The structure is a stack of rooms with a column running through them all from top to bottom of the building. It seems to have been the original intention to carry this palazzo farther north, towards the Palazzo dei Consoli, which would have made it a horizontal contrast to the taller Pretorio.

North out of the Piazza della Signoria the **Via dei Consoli** winds down the hill, one of Gubbio's most interesting streets. On the west are the remains of a tower, and a series of houses with what is called the *porta del morte*, or 'door of the dead'. These tall narrow doors, standing beside the wide doors at street level, are traditionally said to have been used for removing coffins. In fact they were originally the only means of access to the upper floors of these houses. Short ladders would have been used to reach these floors, and pulled up for security. The wide doors at street level would have given access to workshops and stores.

At the Largo del Bargello is a pretty fountain and the

Gubbio: the Palazzo del Bargello.

Gubbio: the Palazzo dei Consoli.

Gubbio: the interior
of the Duomo.

13th-century **Palazzo del Bargello**, much like coeval private palazzi in the city but in a better state of preservation. However, the gulf between this civic building and the complex discussed earlier shows how quickly and radically a city's ambitions, wealth and artistic understanding could change.

From the Via dei Consoli, Via Galeotti, a covered street, winds towards the **Duomo**, an early-14th-century Gothic building with a powerful interior of ten pointed arches supporting the roof. These arches run into pilasters with only the mildest flutter of a capital to intervene, and the effect of the structure illustrates the double meaning of the word *nave* in Italian: 'nave', but also 'ship': here upturned to form a magnificent piece of architecture. Some fragmentary medieval frescoes remain, but most of the work is later.

Beyond Largo del Bargello is Piazza Giordano Bruno, and Via Gabrielli going north, with many 14th-century houses; at the north end (Via Capitano del Popolo) is the **Palazzo del Capitano del Popolo**, built in the late 1200s when that office was instituted. Many of the streets at this northern end of Gubbio are full of medieval interest: Via Cleofe Borromei, Via del Popolo and Borgo Felice Damiani might be mentioned.

The final building of significant interest is at the opposite end of the city, and can be reached by following Via Baldassani and then Via Savelli to Porta Romana. Outside this gate is the church of **Sant'Agostino**, a forerunner of the Duomo, built in the later 13th century. Its scheme of arches is similar, though here they are opposed on the outside by semicircular buttresses, somewhat like those at Assisi. The façade is 20th-century.

**OTHER
TOWNS AND
ISOLATED
BUILDINGS**

Pietralunga, north of the N.219: a town that retains its medieval aspect with many buildings, a parish church – the Pieve de' Saddi – and a complete set of walls.

Montelabate, west of the N.298. The town is dominated by the church of **Santa Maria**, Romanesque-Gothic of about 1325. It belonged to the monastery of Montelabate, a rich foundation which at its height possessed 20 castles and 30 parish churches. Santa Maria has a fine 13th-century cloister and a well-preserved crypt of the 11th century.

Campo Reggiano, N.219. The abbey of Campo Reggiano was built around the middle of the 11th century; it has a crypt with interesting capitals.

Città di Castello, at the junction of the N.3 and the N.221. On the western side of Piazza Matteotti is the **Palazzo del Podestà** (now the Pretura), a vast building attributed to Angelo da Orvieto. The Piazza Matteotti façade is 17th-century, but along Corso Cavour the north flank is in severe Gothic style. Farther along Corso Cavour is Piazza Gabriotti and the **Palazzo Comunale**, built in 1334–52 by Angelo da Orvieto. This two-storey building has many features in common with the Florentine Palazzo Vecchio. There is the same rusticated masonry, voussoir arches and two-light windows. There is a somewhat more rigorous division here between the regularity of the first floor with its line of evenly-spaced windows and the free play of openings on the wall below. A third storey was planned for the Palazzo Comunale but never built. Inside is a vaulted atrium and a ramp leading to the first-floor Sala Maggiore.

Abbazia di Santa Maria di Sitria, north of the N.360: founded in the 11th century by St Romualdo, this is an interesting Romanesque church in splendid surroundings. The crypt is supported by a single column with an antique Corinthian capital. Beside the church is the old cenobium, or group of cells. One of these is called 'the prison of St Romualdo', where the saint was locked up by his fellow monks for a period of six months.

Gualdo Tadino, on the N.3. The town is in a pretty location overlooking a plain, with a recently restored Rocca, built by Frederick II in the 13th century with alterations in 1394. The Gothic church of San Francesco in Corso Italia was consecrated in 1315, a fine building.

THE CENTRE
ASSISI, FOLIGNO, MONTEFALCO, BEVAGNA, SPOLETO, TERNI, NARNI

Assisi had its day as a free commune in the 12th century, a Ghibelline city favoured by Frederick Barbarossa, who stayed here often and lived in Assisi as a child. The city fought the emperor's cause, frequently warring with Perugia, but Barbarossa nevertheless gave Assisi to the Duke of Spoleto. This the citizens would not support, rebelling in 1198, but in the following century they submitted to papal domination, and had a series of *signori*, including the Visconti, Montefeltro and Sforza. The 15th century saw Assisi tangled in civil wars, and subsequently it became a docile fraction of the papal states.

But from an artistic point of view Assisi is San Francesco – St Francis – and the monuments built to his memory and way of life. The saint, born into a wealthy family in 1181 or 1182, intended to become a soldier until in the early years of the 13th century he heard God's voice telling him to 'go and repair my house, which is falling down'. The difference here between St Francis and other wealthy men who turned to the Church is that he did not retire to family land and live alone. On the contrary, St Francis devoted himself to work within society. His first task was in fact to do as he was asked, and he began to repair the three churches of San Damiano, San Pietro and the Porziuncola. He then overcame a naturally strong repugnance of lepers and began to work among them, the symbols and actuality of medieval misfortune. His father, worried by the rate at which his own money was disappearing in these projects and the aberrant behaviour of his son, began the process of drawing up a legal act of disinheritance. But St Francis pre-empted this by renouncing all money and returning even the clothes on his back to his father. Around 1210 he and a dozen companions obtained approval from Innocent III for his

(*Opposite*) Spoleto: San Pietro.

125

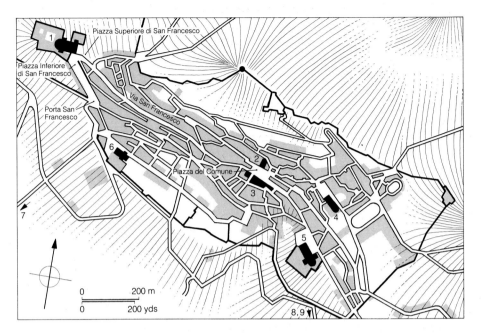

Assisi
1. San Francesco
2. Palazzo del Capitano del Popolo
3. Palazzo Comunale (dei Priori)
4. Duomo
5. Santa Chiara
6. San Pietro
7. Abbazia di San Benedetto
8. San Damiano
9. Santa Maria di Rivotorto

rule, and the order of *Frati Minori*, Minorites, was founded. Two years later his sister Clare (Santa Chiara) initiated the order of *Clarisse*. St Francis travelled widely to preach his message of poverty and humility, received the stigmata at La Verna in 1224, and died in 1226. Feeling the nearness of death he had himself taken to the tiny church of the Porziuncola, and, lying on the bare earth, asked his friends to take care of his 'dearest lady, Poverty'. The bishops of Assisi had to constrain St Francis to wear the clothing he would otherwise have cast off on his death-bed, telling him that, as he owned no possessions, the clothes he wore were not his to give away. He died on the evening of 3 October and was canonized two years later in 1228. The immeasurable effect that St Francis had on medieval society was no less profound in the fields of painting and architecture.

* * *

The position of Assisi is not dissimilar to that of Gubbio, with Mount Subasio to the south-east, and overlooking

126

the Chiáscio-Topino river plain to the west. The town, the greater part of its buildings made from the white and pink limestone quarried from Mount Subasio, is built on artificial terraces that run with the hillside's contours, with narrow winding streets and oddly quiet piazzas. Throughout the town are medieval houses, often with the *porta del morte* that was described in Gubbio, but I will concentrate here on the church of San Francesco.

The 13th-century Porta San Francesco opens slightly east of the church, and the road winds up from there to the Piazza Inferiore di San Francesco, a large and largely desolate piazza, whose arcading was added in the 15th century to provide accommodation for the many pilgrims visiting the church. This piazza provides a good viewpoint to take in the main constituents of this astonishing complex. At the left are the high double arcades that support the conventual buildings on the west (14th-century), designed by Matteo Gattapone. Directly ahead is the double church of **San Francesco** and its campanile, to the right a staircase leading to the upper piazza.

The church was begun in 1228 and consecrated in 1253, though certainly not complete in all its details at that time. The **lower church** in fact was much extended in the late 13th century. Its original form would have corresponded to that of the upper church, the Latin cross with round apse, and a nave without aisles. But side chapels were added and the east end (and remember that the orientation of this church is reversed) extended. The effect is of a great undercroft, neither church-like nor crypt-like, with

Assisi: the upper and lower churches of San Francesco.

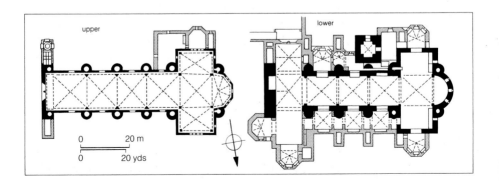

127

its massive round arches spanning laterally and its ceiling vaulted. The ribs are highly decorated and the ceiling painted blue with stars, all work of around 1236, as are the frescoes on either side of the nave. Most of these were destroyed or damaged with the opening of the side chapels. A complete description of the fresco work within the chapels would need a special guide, but it may be worth mentioning at this point something of the history and technique of this type of painting.

Fresco work involves the application of paint to *fresco*, fresh – that is, still wet – plaster. The technique, known in classical days, has the great advantage of durability, because the colours when properly applied react chemically with the plaster as it sets. However it must be put on while the plaster is wet. At Pompeii we find rooms where the plaster is up to 10cm (4in) thick, in order to ensure a long setting period, and therefore allowing the whole room to be plastered at one time and then painted. Medieval work is not as sophisticated as that, being generally applied to plaster of at most 2.5cm (1in) and sometimes as little as 3mm (⅛in) thick. As a result the plaster dried quickly, and only as much plaster could be put on as could be painted in one day. The inferiority of this method lies in the inevitable joints that show up between different days' work, and the overlapping of fresh paint onto dry plaster. Colours, which alter dramatically as the plaster sets, also change according to the plaster mix, and differing qualities of sand, water and lime can all lead to altered tones and shades between one patch and its neighbour.

But then fresco work was initially meant as an inexpensive and quick form of decoration. 'Real' churches were covered in mosaic, and it was only with the explosion of church building in the late Middle Ages that new techniques were found – or rather that these old techniques were re-employed. The artists of Venice and Ravenna were the masters of mosaic who had worked their art throughout Italy, so it is only natural to find that the earliest fresco paintings imitate Byzantine forms. But as so often is the case, what began as an expedient device was worked up by native intelligence into an art form with a unique expressive quality of the highest order.

The **upper church** has a façade, which the lower, being underground, lacks. A steep pediment sits on a square base, which is divided in two by a thin cornice. The upper half has a beautiful rose window, the lower a double entrance door within a single portal. Internally this church shows a more 'advanced' Gothic than the lower, but in its luminosity and proportions shows a complete contrast with it. Here the single space has remained intact, a wonderful balance between height and breadth, vertical and horizontal. There is very little elaboration of structure – even the buttresses that counterthrust the arches are made as simple cylinders running up the outside of the building. It seems clear that the Italian architects recognized in Gothic certain possibilities – a grace of line and a tensioning of surface – that were unavailable in Romanesque architecture. But equally clearly they did not want the pyrotechnics. It has been said before that this was in many ways an architecture in the service of painters, and that is true here more than anywhere else. Transepts and apse are entirely covered here with the work of Cimabue and his assistants, dating from about 1277. Unfortunately the whites of these frescoes have blackened owing to the use of lead oxide. Later fresco works in the nave, the attribution of which is a touchy matter among scholars, are by Jacopo Torriti, Pietro Cavallini and Giotto. Yet they are planned and painted in a way that is integrated to a remarkable extent with the architecture it lies upon, with painted drapery, columns and cornices, not competing with but complementing, extending real space into pictorial space. This had not been done before, and it opened up a new direction in European art.

East from the Piazza Superiore lies the Piazza del Comune, with, in the north-west corner, the **Palazzo del Capitano del Popolo** (13th-century). Nearby is the Torre del Popolo, begun around 1212 and completed in 1305, in the base of which are embedded the measures of standard bricks and tiles in use in 1348. Next to this is the incongruous Temple of Minerva, dating from the early years of the Roman empire and very well preserved. On the south side stands the **Palazzo Comunale** or **dei Priori**,

Assisi: the south-west side of the Piazza del Comune, including the Palazzo Comunale.

built in 1337 and covered with the usual armorial bearings carved in stone. Within is the Pinacoteca Civica.

Via di San Rufino leads east again to Piazza San Rufino and the **Duomo**, begun in 1140 to the designs of Giovanni da Gubbio and carried slowly to its completion in 1253. The façade has affinities with San Francesco in its disposition of forms and its division into three horizontal fields. But here the lower cornice is a small row of arcading, while the pediment at the top is cut by a large pointed arch sitting on pilasters that run to the ground. A large rose window in the centre is flanked by two lesser windows, and the door below it by two lesser doors. The composition reflects very accurately the interior organization of the building, something that Italian architects have not always cared much about (and why should they?). The plan is a basilica with nave and aisles, but the interior was completely rebuilt in the 16th century. Presumably a dome must have been part of the original scheme, and parts of it can still be seen. In the font within the southern aisle were baptized St Francis and his sister St Clare, as well as the Emperor Frederick II in 1197.

South of the Duomo is the Gothic church of **Santa Chiara**, begun in 1257 to much the same pattern in plan and façade as the upper church of San Francesco and completed in 1265. A pink and white striping gives the façade a delicacy not diminished by the three massive flying buttresses attached to the church's north side in the early 14th century to halt structural movement. In fact these additions are in themselves indicative of the Italian attitude to Gothic. Great quadrant arches, they seem less supporting of than supported by the church, too over-balanced to stand alone. Thus their visual independence is declared, and the church left unencumbered. A more 'structurally pure' approach might easily have added bulk and cloyed the whole composition. The interior is frescoed.

The Benedictine church of **San Pietro** stands in its own piazza to the west of the city, a Romanesque-Gothic reconstruction of the early 1200s, completed in 1253. The façade is a variant on that of the Duomo, but lacks the pediment. Not only does the plan have a nave and aisles, but this church has the dome of which only a fragment exists in the Duomo.

The tenth-century Benedictine **Abbazia di San Benedetto**, south-west of the city, was destroyed by the citizens of Assisi in 1399 because it had sheltered their enemies. It is now a ruin, with two very fine crypts. It was this monastery that gave St Francis his little chapel of Porziuncola.

That chapel is now only to be visited by entering the large and vulgar neo-classical church of Santa Maria degli Angeli, built to protect it in 1569. Earthquakes sent to destroy the nave have been answered with yet colder and harsher classicism. The chapel within is a simple 11th-century structure that must have remained the most common type of ecclesiastical building in the 13th and 14th centuries. Near at hand and built in to the new building's structure is the **Cappella del Transito**, where St Francis died. Modern sensibilities will be (or ought to be) shocked at this transformation of a once peaceful wood-land retreat into the hard and pompous interior of a church.

San Damiano, on the southern outskirts of Assisi, where St Francis heard the voice of God instructing him to 'repara domum meam', was in fact restored by the saint,

(*Opposite*) Bevagna: the apse of San Michele.

and still preserves much of its 13th-century character. St Francis acquired the means to repair the church by selling some goods that his father had entrusted to him for the market, and the horse he took them on, at Foligno. But when he presented the money to the priest, the latter declined to take it, and St Francis then threw it out of the window. He later raised the money by begging for it.

Another monument to the simple life is to be found a mile or two further south within the church of **Santa Maria di Rivotorto**, erected in 1854 to replace a 16th-century building that had been put up around the Franciscan 'Tugurio', and was destroyed by an earthquake. *Tugurio* means hovel, and in this simple building, rebuilt but evidently with some archaeological accuracy, St Francis and his two companions Bernardo di Quintavalle and Pietro Cattani first established their order in 1208.

FOLIGNO

Foligno: Santa Maria Infraportas.

Foligno is a pretty town on the Topino river with an unusual **Duomo**, begun in 1133. An impressive façade with three rose windows and open arcading above the main door conceals, unfortunately, a 16th- and 18th-century interior. The **Palazzo Tricini**, to the north-west of the Duomo, was begun in 1389 and has a lovely Gothic staircase, with frescoed walls, and a courtyard. The building is now the civic museum and art gallery. The 11th-century church of **Santa Maria Infraportas** stands in Piazza San Domenico on the west of the city, a fascinating building with a small portico leading to a barrel-vaulted nave, with two aisles cross-vaulted at a later date. On the southern aisle is the 12th-century Cappella dell'Assunta, with frescoes of Byzantine character dating from around 1250.

The nearby Benedictine abbey of **Sassovivo** has a modern church but also an outstanding cloister, built by Pietro de Maria in 1229. The work is remarkable, first because of its pronounced classical aspect, with round-headed arches surmounted by a straight classical cornice, and second because it was prefabricated in Rome and sent here piece by piece. It is made of coloured marbles and decorated with mosaic.

Montefalco has a good battlemented gate in the **Porta Sant'Agostino**, the remaining portion of its 14th-century walls, and a Gothic **church** of the same name nearby (1279–85). The **Cappella di Santa Croce**, adjoining the church of Santa Chiara, is entirely covered in frescoes of around 1333. One of the best panoramic views in Umbria is seen from the top of the **Palazzo Comunale** (1270 but much altered).

· **Bevagna** has a good deal of its 13th- and 14th-century walling, but above all is worth visiting for its **Piazza Silvestri**, surrounded by medieval buildings. The **Palazzo dei Consoli**, with its wide external staircase, is of 1270. **San Silvestro** (1195) is a lovely barn-like Romanesque church that has survived almost intact. Also in the piazza is **San Michele**, built in the late 1100s and early 1200s, with a large rose window above a splendid main door. The interior has been mauled.

MONTEFALCO AND BEVAGNA

Spoleto has the 13th-century **San Domenico**, with a pink and white striped façade and a recently restored interior. **San Paolo inter Vineas** is a restored 12th- and 13th-century church, very classical in tone. Under the church of Sant' Ansano (rebuilt) is the **Crypt of SS Isacco and Marziale**, two Syrian monks who fled persecution in the Near East in the sixth century and settled near Spoleto. The crypt is of the 11th or 12th century. **Sant'Eufemia** is another fine 12th-century church, a basilica with aisles, three apses and a gallery, behind a plain façade.

SPOLETO

The **Duomo**, in spite of alterations, has much of its 12th-century character, including an unusually rich façade (the portico is late 15th-century), with three pointed arches reflecting nave and aisles within (rebuilt in the 15th century), and no less than eight rose windows, five of which are blind.

Dominating the town is the **Rocca**, built to a project by Matteo Gattapone in the 14th century. The plan is rectangular, divided into two sections and with six towers. The Court of Honour inside is a double loggia that very nearly reaches the refined neo-classicism of the following

Spoleto: San Salvatore.

century. The water supply for this fortress, and for the town, came by way of the **Ponte delle Torri** to the south-east, a gigantic ten-light aqueduct, 80m (87½yds) high and 230m (250yds) long, also built by Gattapone.

About a mile south of the city is the fascinating **San Pietro**, a fifth-century church with many rebuildings. Of greatest interest is the 13th-century façade, a collage of relief panels by a variety of sculptors. With its animals, saints and patterning, this is one of the finest examples of Romanesque sculpture in Umbria. The interior was completely rebuilt in 1699.

The basilica of **San Salvatore**, standing just north-east of Spoleto, presents us with a link to church architecture of the fourth and fifth centuries. Here the façade, once faced with marble, has three classical windows at high level, one round-headed and two with pediments and once divided and framed by four pilasters sitting on a straight cornice. Below are three trabeated entrance doors. The plan is basilican, nave and two aisles, with a rounded apse. The interior is largely made up of antique columns, Corinthian and Doric, sometimes with their own capitals; where these were not available, bits were used from various sources to make up the numbers. The ornamentation of this building shows the first influx of oriental influence into Italian art.

TERNI AND NARNI

Terni: San Salvatore.

Terni's **San Salvatore** is a circular Roman temple adapted in the 12th century as a church by the addition of a rectangular nave, executed with wonderful clarity and precision, both in itself and in its relationship with the older building. **Sant'Alò** is an 11th-century Romanesque church. **San Francesco**, designed by Angelo da Orvieto and begun in 1345, is a compact and plain structure of considerable proportional sophistication, with the cylindrical buttressing found at Assisi and elsewhere in Umbria.

The medieval quarter of Terni, east of the piazza Nuovo Mercato, was badly damaged in the last war, but the **Torre dei Castelli** remains, and several other houses, as well as the street layout.

Narni, on the river Nera, is a pretty city with a strong medieval character, in parts. Via Garibaldi has several interesting buildings of the 13th and 14th century, and in the Piazza dei Priori is the **Palazzo del Podestà**, made in the 13th century by the joining together of three tower-houses and subsequently altered in the following two centuries. In the same piazza is the magnificent **Loggia dei Priori**, credited to Gattapone, of the 1300s, and consisting of a thin single-storey slice of building resting on a massive arcade twice its height.

Along Strada Mazzini is the little Romanesque church of **Santa Maria in Pensole**, of 1175, and in the other direction, Via del Monte and other picturesque streets lead towards the **Rocca**, built in 1370 as a papal fortress.

Narni: the doorway and interior of Santa Maria in Pensole.

Abbazia di Sant'Eutizio, 16km (10m) north of Norcia. The present building was begun in 1190 and completed around 1236. A single door is surmounted by a rose window. The locale is associated with St Benedict, who was born in nearby Norcia in the fifth century and apparently spent some time in these hills.

Chiesa di San Salvatore, Campi Vecchio, 10km (6m) north of Norcia. The town has a medieval aspect still. The 14th-century church is a double-nave affair, with a single pitch roof but two rose windows and an entrance door below each, one for each nave: a charming building.

Abbazia di San Pietro in Valle, off the N.209, 20km (12m) north-east of Terni: a wonderful representative of the medieval monastery, begun in the eighth century – in the church the apse and transepts remain – and altered and added to until the 12th. The church has frescoes from the late 1100s, showing the Umbrian artists working in the Byzantine style. The monastery's campanile and cloister are of the 1300s, the latter particularly fine.

OTHER TOWNS AND ISOLATED BUILDINGS

Abbazia di San Pietro in Valle.

135

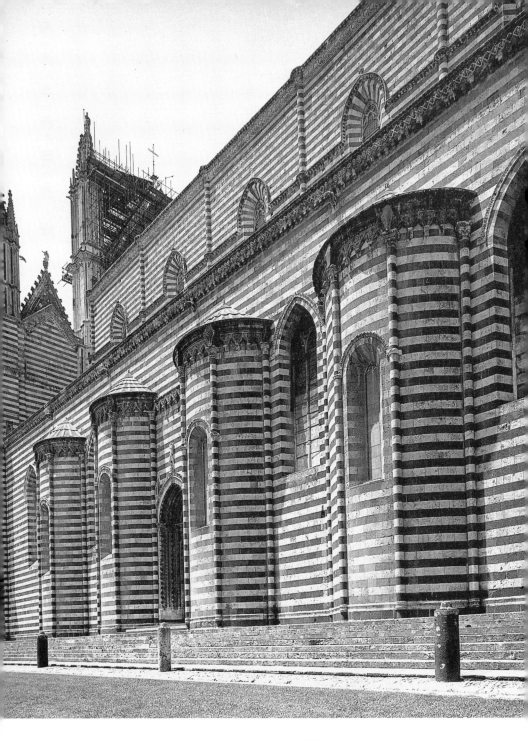

THE WEST
ORVIETO AND TODI

Orvieto is built on a large and isolated platform of volcanic tufa, sitting above its surrounding plain like a great stranded ark. And indeed its distance from the sea became the city's great problem during late medieval times. With the formation of a commune in the 11th and 12th centuries, Orvieto was in a position to look for a port, vital for a city more dependent on industry than on banking, and whose *contado* was not perhaps as rich as those of the more western cities. Amidst civil wars between the families of Monaldeschi (Guelph) and Filippeschi (Ghibelline), wars were fought with Siena and Viterbo, Todi and Perugia, and alliances formed with Florence and Rome. The coastal city of Orbetello belonged to it on and off, until taken into Sienese hands in 1414. The first half of the 14th century saw the defeat of the Filippeschi and the subsequent splitting of the Monaldeschi into two opposing camps. The pattern is familiar from many other central Italian cities at this time, as is the resulting history of numerous *signori* in the latter 1300s and the complete submission to papal authority that eventually followed.

The city shows a clear division into religious, political and administrative centres, developed in the 13th and 14th centuries along the main axis and commercial artery, the Via della Mercanzia (now Corso Cavour/Via della Cava) that runs east to west from one end of the city to the other.

Around the site of the Roman Forum – the present Piazza della Repubblica, and the medieval Piazza Maggiore – buildings were bought up and demolished in the 1200s to make way for the Palazzo Comunale (replaced in the 16th century). Later in the same century the Palazzo del Popolo was built to the north-east, while to the south-east, religious buildings gravitated to the Piazza del Duomo, where a cathedral had stood long before the

(Opposite) Orvieto: detail of the southern wall of the Duomo.

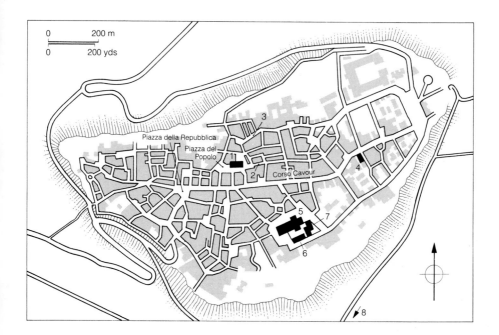

present building was put up in the 1290s. Walls were never needed to defend this city, surrounded as it is by vertical cliffs. The Rocca dominating the city at the east end of Via Cavour was begun in 1364 to enforce Orvieto's loyalty to the pope, though later ruined and restructured on several occasions.

The magnificent **Palazzo del Popolo**, built of warm, honey-golden tufa, was begun in 1157 as the Palazzo Apostolico. It was given to the commune by the pope in the mid-13th century, when the office of Capitano del Popolo was created: an expression of the city's new administrative functions in the hands of the guild and merchant class. The original building was made to a pattern more common in northern than central Italy, with a ground floor consisting of an open loggia, acting as a screen to separate two piazzas (del Popolo and Vivaria), a large meeting room above, and offices above that. In 1280 alterations were made that gave the structure its present form: a bell-tower and new room, the *Caminata*, were added, the external stair was reduced in size, and the ground-level arches were closed up. The fact that there is some uncertainty about which parts date from which building period only confirms the ability of medieval artists to understand and extend the continuity of a work of art, as well as the value of an architecture based on asymmetrical massing. The Romanesque-Gothic of the building is peculiar to Orvieto, evident in details like the corbelled arches of the balcony, the chequerboard decoration, and the curly merlons of the battlements.

Leading from the Piazza del Popolo, **Via Arnolfo di Cambio** is flanked by medieval houses: Nos.4–6 and 10–14 are particularly good. North of Piazza Vivaria, Nos.6–12 **Via della Pace** are also worth seeing, as is the group of artisans' houses at Nos.248–50 Corso Cavour, near the small Romanesque church of **Santo Stefano**.

South of Via Cavour is the Piazza del Duomo, and what is unquestionably one of the great works of Italian architecture, the **Duomo** itself. The story of its building starts in the year 1263, with a Bohemian priest stopping to celebrate mass at nearby Bolsena while on his way from Prague to Rome. The priest, it seems, had doubts about transubstantiation. Yet on this occasion the host he raised to his lips turned bloody, staining the corporal-cloth and liturgical vestments. Naturally – or unnaturally – upset, the priest ran to Orvieto, where Pope Urban IV was

Orvieto: the Palazzo del Popolo.

Orvieto: Duomo
1. Cappella del
   Corporale
2. Cappella Nuova

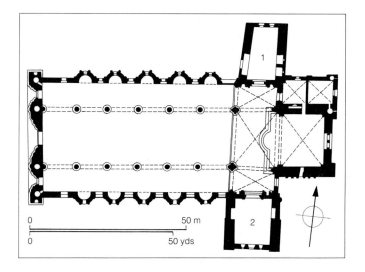

living, and told his tale. The pope despatched Bishop Giacomo to Bolsena to confirm the truth of this story, and his messenger returned with the bloody cloths themselves. This was surely a stroke of heavenly intervention, for Orvieto at that time was infested with Patarine heretics, whose principal heterodoxy was the dismissal of transubstantiation as a fiction. The blood-stained cloths were shown to the people, the feast of Corpus Domini added to the calendar, and the heretics routed. All of this seemed, especially to the Orvietan bishop Francesco di Bagnioregio, to call for some special kind of building.

The cathedral was built in three main phases: nave, transepts and then façade. Pope Nicholas IV laid the foundation stone of the new cathedral on 13 November 1290. The original plan was for a Romanesque basilica, with nave and aisles and a semicircular apse, possibly to designs of Arnolfo di Cambio but under the supervision of Fra' Bevignate of Perugia. The nave was built to this plan, but in 1300 the work was taken over by an Orvieto man, Giovanni di Uguccione, who carried on the work in Gothic style, substituting stone vaulting for open-truss roofing. The vaulting led to the walls giving way, and the advice was sought, around 1305, of Lorenzo Maitani of Siena, who stabilized the walls with four lateral flying buttresses and squared up the apse, placing in it the present traceried east window. Maitani also designed and began to construct (1310–30) a scheme for the façade. Of the successors to the Sienese master the most noteworthy are Nicolò and Meo Nuti (1331–47), Andrea Pisano (1347–8), and Andrea Orcagna (1359). Around 1350 the **Cappella del Corporale** was inserted between the flying buttresses on the north side, and in 1408 the **Cappella Nuova** in the corresponding position on the south.

The most interesting part of this work is without doubt the nave of the original project, with its extraordinary asymmetries and visual dynamics. The whole is made of alternating stripes of tufa and basalt, yellow and grey rather than black and white, producing a much less harsh result than the walls of Siena, and reminiscent of the subtle walling at Pisa. The nave is simple, with a high roof and plain clerestory windows. The undersides of its arches are curved, so acting almost as elastic extensions of the round columns from which they spring. The result of this tranquillity in the nave is an opening up of the aisles, and it is here that the formal asymmetries begin. Each wall contains five semicircular apses, which would have been minor variants of the major recess at the east end of the church, separated by a window. But neither window nor niche is centred between columns. Nor, when the nave is looked at more closely, are the clerestory windows. The rippling sense of space produced by aisle walls and nave arches as you move down the nave is something unique in architecture.

The façade begun by Maitani in 1310 was carried on by Andrea Pisano and later Andrea Orcagna, who designed the magnificent rose window around 1359. Here is the façade that Siena's cathedral in its later stages was trying to copy. Here the organization is clear, and strong enough to support the incredible richness of sculpture and mosaic decorations that cover its every square foot. Four tall piers divide the front into two minor and a major central space. The heavy surface of the lower level undulates in and out between the three entrance doors, above which rise three gables. A line of arcading runs at the top of these gables, acting as a base for two more lateral gables and Orcagna's

Orvieto: the façade
of the Duomo.

rose window (a feature foreseen by Maitani). Finally, the central bay is crowned with a nearly equilateral gable. The mosaics that fill up all the flat surfaces were replaced in the 18th century, with the exception of the *Nativity of Mary*, in the gable over the south door, made in 1364 and restored in 1713 and 1786. Seen at evening the golden mosaics light up like fire in the sun, and the architectural and sculptural elements seem to come alive.

Beside the Duomo stands the **Palazzo Soliano**, or **Palazzo dei Papi**, begun in 1297 by Boniface VIII, presumably to replace the Palazzo Apostolico given to the commune a generation earlier. The first floor is entirely taken up with a single vaulted hall, reached by a wide staircase and balcony.

At the end of the piazza to the right of the Duomo is the **Palazzo Papale**, built in the 13th century, recently restored and turned into a museum.

About two miles from Orvieto to the south is the ruined **Abbazia dei SS Severo e Martirio**. The old church was built in the early 1100s, as was the lovely polygonal belfry. Much of the rest was erected in the first half of the 13th century, after the monks were expelled from the Benedictine rule for disobedience to the local bishop and the abbey given to the French Premonstratensians.

Within its walls, part Etruscan, part Roman and part medieval, Todi remains a city of tortuous streets, rich in medieval detail and monuments. At its highest point is the long rectangular Piazza Vittorio Emanuele II, on the site of the Roman Forum. In medieval times this piazza was closed by four gates, removed in the 16th century. Four superb monumental buildings combine to make this piazza one of the finest in central Italy: the Palazzo dei Priori, Palazzo del Popolo, Palazzo del Capitano, and the Duomo, all begun in the 13th century.

TODI

The **Palazzo del Popolo** is the earliest in the series, an austere building in northern Gothic style begun in 1213, with a storey added in 1228. It is tall and narrow, with an arcade at ground level and two widely separated rows of arched window groups above. The south side of the building, facing Piazza Garibaldi, shows signs of the original staircase to the first floor, and the old entrance door. But these were replaced in the 1290s when the **Palazzo del Capitano** was built next to it on the north.

This building is lower and has been set back relative to the earlier building, and in the re-entrant space a broad staircase has been built giving access to both. The style has changed, a more ample and confident architecture replacing the fortress-like qualities of the Palazzo del Popolo. There is a ground floor of two great arches, and at first-floor level a triplet of three-light windows and gables on the left balances an off-centre entrance door lower down on the right, while high above are four groups of similar windows beneath segmental arches, uniformly

143

spread across the façade. Battlements are replaced by a projecting roof. As at the Orvieto Palazzo del Popolo, the most sensitive architectural skill has gone into this union of old and new, from the wonderful massing relationships to the detail of the windows.

South of this group is the **Palazzo dei Priori**, begun in 1293, enlarged and completed in 1334. The Palazzo was first the residence of the Podestà, then of the Priori, and finally of the Rettori, the papal governors. The building's mass maintains the medieval actuality of the square, although the Gothic windows were stripped out in 1513 and replaced by Renaissance types.

Opposite this palazzo, at the top of a great flight of 29 steps, stands the **Duomo**. The church of SS Annunziata was begun in the early 1100s but not carried through to completion until the 16th century, when the large rose window was inserted in the façade. The rest of the façade is from the 13th century. Its three entrance doors and two small rose windows on the lower level, and division into three by pilasters, make it somewhat reminiscent of the Assisi churches. This is borne out by the interior, and confirms the connexion: both this and the Assisi churches owe significant elements to contemporary French Gothic.

South of the Piazza Vittorio Emanuele II, in the Piazza della Repubblica, is a more remarkable church, also standing at the top of a long flight of steps, and also with a debt to the same source. The Franciscan church of **San Fortunato** was begun in 1292, and much of it completed by 1328, although the western half was only finished in the 15th century. The lower half of its incomplete façade is similar to that of the Duomo. A pitched roof spreading the full width of the façade is the only hint that things will be different inside – but how different they are! Nave and aisles are here of equal height, all vaulted on slender columns that are virtually clusterings together of the roof's vault ribs. Opening off the aisles – half the width of the nave – are deep side chapels, two per bay, entered through heavy pointed arches. The high-level windows of the outside walls have been blocked off, but even now the space has an extraordinary lightness. The proliferation of side chapels in Franciscan churches seems to owe some-

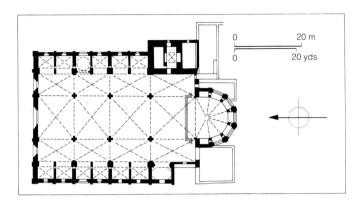

Todi: San Fortunato.

thing to the patronage of wealthy families, demanding their own monumental 'quarters' and, for a price, getting them. By raising the aisle roofs and giving such a strongly architectural ordering to these side chapels – which in many churches became a rag-bag of architectural clutter – the directionality normally associated with churches dissolves, and east-west becomes as significant as north-south (the altar of this church is on the south).

There are many medieval houses to be seen in Todi. The **Borgo Nuovo**, a medieval 'suburb' outside the Roman walls, slopes steeply (and picturesquely) down to the Porta Perugia, standing among medieval walls and towers.

Panicale, north of the N.220: the town has a very pretty medieval quarter, partly walled and entered by a medieval gate.

Castiglione del Lago, jutting into Lago Trasimeno: the town has battlemented medieval walls and towers, and many buildings of the period.

OTHER
TOWNS AND
ISOLATED
BUILDINGS

FURTHER READING

Good general histories of Italy in the Middle Ages are *A Short History of Italy*, edited by H. Hearder and D.P. Waley, Cambridge, 1963; *Society and Politics in Medieval Italy: The Evolution of the Civil Life, 1000–1350*, J.K. Hyde, London, 1973; *Culture and Society in Italy 1290–1420*, John Larner, London, 1971. *The Italian City-Republics*, 3rd edition, Daniel Waley, London and New York, 1988, is more specific about political developments in central Italy.

For more architectural and artistic issues: *Art and Architecture in Italy: 1250–1400*, John White, London, 1966, excellent art-historical writing, lively and penetrating. Kenneth J. Conant's *Carolingian and Romanesque Architecture: 800–1200*, London, 1966, is a good book that unfortunately finds little place for a discussion of Italian developments. *The Building of Renaissance Florence*, Richard A. Goldthwaite, Baltimore and London, 1990, looks at the nuts-and-bolts building of the city, and although dealing mainly with the 15th century, is full of insights into traditional construction practice.

General surveys of medieval architecture and urbanism in Italy are not very well covered by English texts. Books such as Mumford's *The City in History*, London, 1961, good as it is, jumps around from the Netherlands to Italy to France, and makes it hard to pin down a thesis to a place. But this is a difficulty inherent in medieval history, when what is true for one city is wrong about another, often when the two are only miles apart. Howard Saalman's *Medieval Cities*, London, 1968, shares this fault and adds one or two more, being wholly dedicated to the thesis that the city is an economic entity and little else: an easy read. A better understanding of the society will be had from *The Fontana*

Economic History of Europe, The Middle Ages, ed. Carlo Cipolla, London, 1972, and vol. II of *A History of Technology*, ed. Charles Singer et al., Oxford, 1956.

Of the guide books, Augustus Hare's *Cities of Central Italy*, 2 vols., London, 1891, much favoured by the *Companion Guide* writers, is out of date in spite of one or two good anecdotes. Hare is better when dealing with a single city than when cataloguing many small ones. The Collins *Companion Guides* themselves are very general and not really useful for architectural study.

The Italian texts are, as one might expect, much better. *Italia Comunale*, Luigi Salvatorelli, Storia d'Italia, vol. IV, Milan, 1940, and *L'Italia nell'età comunale*, Antonio Viscardi and Gianluigi Barni, Società e Costume, vol. IV, Turin, 1966, are both intelligent, readable books, with good illustrations, dealing with medieval culture and society in all its manifestations. Paolo Favole's *Piazze d'Italia*, Milan, 1972, is a picture book with extended captions and an introductory essay, providing a survey of the development of the piazza throughout Italy from earliest times to the present. Several individual cities have so far been given volumes of their own, variable in quality, in Laterza's *Le città nella storia d'Italia* series, and many more are planned. These give a run-down of the urban and architectural history of each city. Enrico Guidoni's *La città dal medioevo al rinascimento*, Bari, 1989, is a good survey with some detailed analysis, not confined to Italian cities.

The Touring Club Italiano publishes excellent guide books, with useful background information, in its Guida d'Italia series: *Toscana (non compresa Firenze)*, 4th edition, Milan, 1974; *Firenze e dintorni*, 6th edition, Milan, 1974; *Umbria*, 5th edition, Milan, 1978.

GLOSSARY

arte guild.

bargello chief constable, often the name of this officer's official residence.

campo santo burial ground; literally: sacred field.

capitano del popolo commander of the local militia.

cardo one of the two axes of a Roman city or military post.

clerestory the upper part of the nave, choir and transepts of a church, containing windows to light the centre of the building.

comune the government of a city-state; a commune.

condottiere a soldier of fortune in command of troops, usually mercenary.

console councillor or adviser.

contado that countryside possessed by a city-state.

contrada a city quarter.

crossing the space in a church formed by the intersection of nave, transepts and chancel.

decumanus one of the two axes of a Roman city or military post.

forestiero an outsider or foreigner.

gonfaloniere standard-bearer, military official.

podestà an official selected from outside the city by the commune. His purpose was to arbitrate in local disputes.

signore, signoria lord, lordship; the feudal ruler of a city. In the context of this book, the signori were the men who imposed tyrannical rule on the republican communes.

torri powerful landowners who built houses within the city walls. So called because these houses were fortified with high towers (*torri*).

vault *barrel vault*: a vault of curved section; *groin-vault*: produced by the intersection of two barrel vaults; *rib-vault*: a groin-vault with the addition of ribs on the diagonal lines of intersection.

voussoir a wedge-shaped stone used in the construction of arches.

CHRONOLOGY

350	Constantinople founded as the second capital of the Roman Empire	
402	Invasion of Italy by the Goths	
476	Last of the Western emperors – Romulus Augustulus – deposed	
529	Benedictine rule established	
568	Lombard invasion of Italy	
751	Ravenna falls to the Lombards, collapse of Byzantine power in North Italy	
754 & 756	Franks under Pepin enter Italy	

at the request of Pope Stephen III

774	Frankish king Charlemagne conquers Lombard kingdom
800	Charlemagne crowned emperor by pope in Rome
875–962	Italian kingdom in decline, power passing to bishops and nobility
962	Otto I of Saxony, crowned emperor in Rome
1059	Baptistry of San Giovanni at

	Florence consecrated	1222–88	Cistercian abbey built at San Galgano
1064	Foundation of Pisan cathedral; Pisan ships successfully raid Palermo	1226	Death of St Francis
		1228–53	Church of San Francesco built at Assisi
1076	Investiture Contest splits papacy (Hiderbrand: Gregory VII) and emperor (Henry IV), creating a power vacuum in the cities and allowing the communes to take root	1245	Excommunication of Frederick II
		1250	Frederick II dies
		1257–65	Church of Santa Chiara built at Assisi
1081–5	Consuls establish authority in Pisa	1260	Florence defeated at the battle of Montaperti; beginning of Ghibelline hegemony in Tuscany
1097–9	Pisan (and Genoese) fleets support the crusades in the Near East and establish trading colonies there	c.1262	Campo at Siena laid out
		1266	Extinction of the Hohenstaufen line with the death of Conradin at Tagliacozzo
1111	Pisa granted free-trade rights (reduced duties) throughout Byzantine Empire	c.1275	Silk-working machinery introduced
1115	Countess Matilda of Tuscany dies, having given her lands (Tuscany) to the Church; disputes for this land between pope and emperor begin	c.1277	Fontana Maggiore built at Perugia
		1278–83	Campo Santo built at Pisa
		1284	Pisans defeated at Meloria by the Genoese
1125	Death of Henry V marks decline of imperial power in Italy	1284–1341	Palazzo Pubblico built at Siena
c.1140	San Michele begun at Lucca		
c.1150	Efficient draught-harness for horses introduced	1290–1408	Orvieto cathedral built
c.1150	Siena Cathedral begun	1293–7	Palazzo dei Priori built at Perugia
1153	Baptistry begun at Pisa		
1155	Frederick Barbarossa crowned emperor	1295–1301	Blacks and Whites at civil war in Florence
1173	Belfry (Leaning Tower) begun at Pisa	c.1294–1390	Santa Croce built at Florence
c.1180	Introduction of stern-post rudder in ships	1296	Arnolfo di Cambio begins the new cathedral at Florence
1190	Death of Barbarossa	1299–1302	Oldest section of the Palazzo della Signoria built at Florence
1198	Innocent III elected pope, foundation of papal states in central Italy	1301	Whites expelled from Florence
		1322–49	Palazzo dei Consoli, Palazzo Pretorio, Piazza della Signoria all built at Gubbio
c.1200	Wheelbarrow introduced in agriculture and building		
c.1200–1220	Political divisions according to Guelphs (supporters of the pope) and Ghibellines (supporters of the emperor) become common in central Italy	c.1323	Santa Maria della Spina completed at Pisa
		1329	Lucca sold by German mercenaries
1201	Fibonacci writes a treatise on the commercial use of Arabic numerals	c.1340	Artillery introduced into European warfare
		1342	Walter de Brienne appointed Signore of Florence; ejected the following year
1209	Franciscan rule approved by Innocent III		
1220	Frederick II crowned emperor	1342–5	Bank failures in Florence (Peruzzi, Bardi and others)

ACKNOWLEDGEMENTS

The publishers would particularly like to thank James Morris for the special photography he undertook for the book.

The photographs are from the following sources: James Morris, London: cover picture, pages 19, 39, 40, 41, 42, 43, 44, 46, 61, 66, 68, 70, 73, 76, 77, 78, 82 top, 82 below, 83, 92, 94, 96 top, 96 below, 97, 98, 100, 101, 103, 106 top, 106 below, 110, 114, 116, 117, 121 top, 122, 124, 130, 132, 133, 134 top, 134 below, 135 top, 135 below, 136, 139. A. F. Kersting, London: pages 26, 29, 30, 32, 35, 38, 53, 58, 59, 60, 84, 93 below, 142. The Mansell Collection, London: pages viii, 4, 11, 121 below, 127. Scala, Florence: pages 14 top, 14 below, 17, 23. Wim Swaan: pages 51, 54, 93 top. Paul Grant, London: frontispiece (page vi). Biblioteca Laurenziana, Florence: page 5.

INDEX

150